The Ten
Commandments
of Dating

Student Edition

The Ten Commandments of Dating

Student Edition

Ben Young

and

Sam Adams

NELSON BOOKS
A Division of Thomas Nelson Publishers
Since 1798

www.thomasnelson.com

Published in Nashville, Tennessee, by Thomas Nelson, Inc.

Unless otherwise noted, Scripture quotations are from The Holy Bible, *New Century Version,* copyright © 1987, 1988, 1991, by W Publishing Group, a division of Thomas Nelson, Inc. Used by permission.

Scripture quotations noted NKJV are from THE NEW KING JAMES VERSION. Copyright © 1979, 1980, 1982, Thomas Nelson, Inc., Publishers. Used by permission. All rights reserved.

Scripture quotations noted NIV are from the HOLY BIBLE: NEW INTERNATIONAL VERSION ®. Copyright © 1973, 1978, 1984 by International Bible Society. Used by permission of Zondervan Publishing House. All rights reserved.

Scripture quotations noted NASB are from the NEW AMERICAN STANDARD BIBLE®, © Copyright The Lockman Foundation 1960, 1962, 1968, 1971, 1972, 1973, 1975, 1977. Used by permission. (www.Lockman.org)

Library of Congress Cataloging-in-Publication Data

Young, Ben.
    The ten commandments of dating / Ben Young and Sam Adams.—Student ed.
       p. cm.
    "Adapted from the original book . . . revised to address the needs of a younger audience, age sixteen and up"—Introd.
    Includes bibliographical references.
    ISBN 0-7852-6059-5 (pbk.)
    1. Dating (Social customs) 2. Dating (Social customs)—Religious aspects—Christianity. 3. Interpersonal relations in adolescence. 4. Sexual ethics for teenagers. I. Adams, Sam. II. Title.
HQ801.Y68 2004
646.7'7—dc22
                                         2004004951

Printed in the United States of America

05 06 07 08 RRD 5

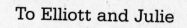

To Elliott and Julie

Contents

Introduction

O ur vision in writing this book is simple: we want to give you the truth about relationships and provide you with ten time-tested laws to protect you and others from the pitfalls of modern dating. Let's face it, we live in a permissive culture. Most of the messages you're getting from magazines and music lyrics about dating relationships are way off base. Do you really think Britney Spears or the people at Abercrombie & Fitch are interested in offering you healthy guidance on this subject? We think not! Worse yet, most TV sitcoms and Hollywood movies give a distorted view of love and romance. We want you to understand what is realistic about relationships at this stage in your life.

For over fifteen years we have worked with young people, students, and singles on how to build good, solid dating relationships. We have spent countless hours listening to you in the counseling office, on Ben's radio show, or during dating conferences, and one theme stands out—dating is risky business. Therefore, it's well worth the effort to do it right. In this book you will discover the secrets to having stable, happy relationships without all the heartache and pain. It's kind of like we're giving you the answers to the SAT before you even take the test (or during the test, if you happen to already be in a relationship).

The difference is that you won't be cheating if you copy the answers and apply them to your life!

Keep in mind that these commandments are not suggestions or recommendations based upon surveys or opinion polls. These are solid truths that, for the most part, have a moral foundation. And just like with the laws of nature, when you break the laws of dating, you experience consequences. On the other hand, when you keep these laws (or commandments), you will be blessed, and your relationships will run more smoothly.

We want to challenge you to seriously consider these relational laws. We suspect that much of your dating confusion can be eliminated if you simply keep these ten relational commandments. Remember, God gave Israel the Ten Commandments to show them how to live life. These ten laws are designed to show you how to interact in your relationships with the opposite sex. Each chapter will spell out the benefits of keeping a commandment and consequences of breaking it. If you've already broken a few, don't panic. You can follow the commandment and get back on track. It's never too late.

Finally, it should be noted that this book has been adapted from the original book (for single adults) and has been revised to address the needs of a younger audience, age sixteen and up. As you venture out into the world of dating, keep in mind that for now it should be fun and lighthearted—a way to get to know the opposite sex and enjoy companionship. Remember: you're young! You have many years of dating ahead of you. Rather than getting wrapped up in serious, exclusive dating relationships, use the wisdom from these commandments to help you establish good habits as you form relationships with the opposite sex. If you keep these commandments, you will experience a greater depth of love, peace, and fulfillment in your own life and in your relationships. You have everything to gain and nothing to lose—so get reading!

Thou Shalt Get a Life

I t's 4:00 on a Friday afternoon, and you've got the whole weekend ahead of you. You grab something to eat and plop down in front of your computer to check your e-mail. As you scroll through the junk mail and the billionth ad for a GAP clearance sale, your cell phone suddenly rings—it's your boyfriend of two months. Anticipating plans for a fun night out, you eagerly answer in your sweetest voice, "Hello?"

"Um, hey." He doesn't sound nearly as excited to be talking to you.

You exchange small talk about the day, and then he proceeds to tell you that he's going out with some of his guy friends tonight and that he'll try to remember to call you tomorrow.

"What do you mean 'you'll try'?" you fire back. "Anyway, I thought we had plans for tonight!"

"Listen, I'm pretty busy these days, and . . . well, I just don't know if I have time for a girlfriend. Maybe we should think about just being friends."

"Whatever . . . I'm busy too. Have a nice time with your friends." You hang up on him, hoping you left him thinking that you couldn't care less what he does with his life or who he spends it with. But inside, your heart sinks into your stomach as you realize that this person, in whom you've invested so much time, energy, and emotion, has just put an end to something you hoped would last forever—well, at least longer than two months. You sit there, staring at your phone, thinking, *He's gonna call back any second and want to talk it out, or maybe tell me he was just plain wrong.* You keep staring at it as seconds tick by. Nothing. You feel hurt, rejected, mad, and all alone.

You spend most of the weekend on the couch, watching re-runs of *That '70s Show* on TV. By Sunday night, for some strange reason, you don't feel any better. In fact, you are still stuck in the same emotional ditch you fell into Friday afternoon when you got the call. You replay the conversation over and over in your head and ask yourself, "What went wrong? Why did something that seemed so good not work out?"

Finally, a startling truth begins to emerge. You had told him you have a busy life too, but suddenly you realize that just isn't true. The truth is, you don't have a life. *This person* was your life. Your entire self-worth was wrapped up in someone else. You now see how you had put your life on hold—your school, family, interests, friends, and even your relationship with God. And now that it's over, you have nothing to sustain you—no one to call, nothing to do. Without your sweetheart, you have no life.

Okay, so maybe this illustration is a bit depressing, but believe us, we have witnessed far too many scenarios just like it. Thousands of people make bad relationship choices and end up with a lot of unnecessary pain because they ignore this first and foundational relationship commandment: Thou Shalt Get a Life!

Years ago the girl of my (Ben's) dreams dumped me

> **People with lives do not have to be dating someone to feel good about themselves.**

twice within a six-week period. Although it felt like she had torn my heart right out of my rib cage, it turned out to be one of the most valuable experiences of my dating life. It was through that double-dumping that I learned that I needed a life. A *real* life! When you invest all your energy and self-esteem in getting a date or having a serious relationship, you have nothing else to give.

People with lives are not sitting around waiting to be swept off their feet. People with lives do not make "getting a boyfriend or girlfriend" their ultimate goal. People with lives do not have to be dating someone to feel good about themselves. People with lives are not always on the prowl, going places and hanging out with certain people just so they can meet a cute guy or a hot girl. Relationships with the opposite sex are important (why else would you be reading this book?), but they must be kept in perspective. When relationships with the opposite sex become too serious or become an obsession, you've got a problem.

> **When relationships with the opposite sex become an obsession, you've got a problem.**

Here's a reality check: if you don't have a life of your own (or get one real soon), you won't be happy, and you certainly won't be someone people will want to spend time with. Why? Because you will have no sense of self-worth, and you will end up sucking the life out of your friends. Inevitably, you will put extraordinary expectations on people to fulfill you, complete you, entertain you, and soothe you. No created thing—certainly no human—can perform up to those outlandish expectations. Only the Creator who made you can do that, and He made you to . . . get a life!

Before you ever even look at the opposite sex again, please follow this first and greatest commandment to get a life. If you are wondering what a real life looks like or how to get one, read on. But first, let's see what can happen when someone decides to rebel and break this first law of relationships. We call it the un-life.

The Un-Life

People who are living the un-life have one thing in common: they have put their lives on hold. They have become so consumed with finding someone to meet their needs and give them a sense of significance that real living has taken a backseat. Some un-lifers just withdraw completely and give up. They have convinced themselves that life isn't worth pursuing with any sort of passion if they don't have a boyfriend or girlfriend. Whether they are obsessed with finding *The One* or are completely jaded to the thought because their hearts have been broken, these are the ones who have contracted the fatal disease of the un-life. Here are the most common symptoms of the un-life, known as the four Deadly Ds.

1. Desperation

A desperate person has a sense of urgency about finding someone to go out with. He is starving for someone to fill the emotional hole in his soul. These desperate people go to places, including youth group functions, only to check out the girls or become friends with so-and-so because her brother is good-looking. Unfortunately their urge-to-merge strategy inevitably hits a dead end: they end up using people, having a miserable time, developing a bad reputation, and scaring off the person they hoped to attract in the first place. Take it from Confucius, the philosopher: "Desperation produces perspiration, and perspiration stinks on anybody."

2. Dependence

A dependent person gains a sense of significance and security through others. She must be attached to someone in order to feel good about herself. We've seen countless people hang on to sick relationships, even emotionally and physically abusive relationships, for this reason.

Ashley, an all-star soccer player, was assertive and unstoppable on the field, but when it came to guys she was as limp as a wet noodle. Her boyfriend had broken up with her, and she seemed unable to make decisions for herself without him. To top it off, she confessed that he was a jerk toward her friends and often was controlling and critical toward her. Now he had changed his mind and wanted to woo her back with all sorts of promises about treating her better. Unbelievable as it may sound, Ashley was thinking about taking him back, and probably would have, had her parents and friends not cautioned her otherwise. We have tremendous compassion for people like Ashley, and we hold out much hope for them to avoid abusive relationships.

Dependent people have difficulty making decisions and taking responsibility for their own lives. When a dependent person enters a relationship, he usually sucks the lifeblood out of the other person like a tick on a dog. Of course, as humans we all depend on others to some degree for certain needs. This is normal and healthy. But a person infected with the un-life will be excessively dependent on the other person to meet most of his or her needs and provide a sense of identity.

3. Depression and Loneliness

Feelings of depression and loneliness are the number one complaint of people who buy into the notion that someone else can make them happy. This can take many forms, but generally it is a condition that affects the whole person: physically, emotionally, and spiritually. Most people living the un-life will experience such conditions as unhappiness, gloom, lack of energy, and withdrawal from others. It is also not uncommon to experience a significant drop in self-esteem.

Because Chad had failed two classes, his GPA dropped too low for him to play varsity basketball or go out for the swim team. His parents were on his case, his teachers had given up on him, and his friends . . . well, they were all busy playing sports. He sought comfort in the arms of his cheerleader girlfriend, Christi, but she soon broke up with him because it was just too depressing to be around him. Needless to say, Chad was seriously bummed. With nothing else to do but study or hang out online, he chose the latter. Immersing himself more and more in the Internet, Chad cut himself off from normal conversation and turned his room into a cave. Rage and distorted views of reality ensued, so that when Chad made an occasional step back into the real world, he was a social black hole. Few people wanted to be around him. This only made him feel worse, and soon his life consisted mostly of surfing the Net, visiting chat rooms, and watching TV. He was caught in a vicious cycle: the more time he spent alone, the less he felt like being with people, and the more his grades suffered.

The danger in depression and loneliness is that it may begin a downward spiral. In other words, the more depressed you feel, the more likely you are to withdraw and exacerbate the situation. Eventually, this can lead to an even worse condition—clinical depression, which can involve symptoms such as loss of appetite and sleep, difficulty with concentration, problems with normal functioning, and feelings of hopelessness. This more severe form of depression calls for professional intervention such as counseling or therapy, and possibly medication.

The good news is that even in the downward spiral a person can be treated and begin a reverse spiral back to having a life. Thanks to his attentive parents who intervened, Chad went to a counselor and got some help. Eventually, he restored his grades and, more important, his relationships with friends and family. Having discarded the un-life, Chad now experiences the joy of living a life that brings happiness to those around him.

4. Detachment

Descriptions like "isolated," "withdrawn," "lonely," and "plays X Box 24/7" describe someone who has disengaged himself from life. The desire to spend time with friends, get involved at school, or serve in the youth group and form other vital social relationships has vanished.

Britney was one of the most outgoing, popular people you could ever meet. However, after her parents' divorce and a rejection letter from the college she wanted, she began to withdraw, feeling like no one understood what she was going through . . . except her boyfriend, Billy. It seemed to her that everything in her life was unstable, except for their relationship. In an effort to avoid another disappointment, she gave up on college altogether and poured her life into Billy. She believed that he was the only good thing in her life, so when he dumped her for her best friend, she was absolutely devastated. Her efforts to escape the pain in her life had totally backfired, and she felt completely hopeless. She began ignoring her friends and distancing herself from family members. In short, she completely isolated herself from everyone to avoid further rejection. I'm sure Britney did not deliberately set out to withdraw so completely, yet it can be easy for anyone to do once they start down this path.

Coping with the Un-Life: Media-Bation

In our high-tech society, one of the biggest dangers for un-lifers is the tendency to use certain forms of media to cope with the isolation. This is what we call *media-bation*. People who look to the media as their primary (or only) source for meeting emotional and relational needs definitely need to get a life. They rely upon the television, radio, video, or the Internet for fulfillment. *Media-bators* spend all their time in front of a screen, at Blockbuster, in a chat room, or at the local CD exchange. A vast subculture has arisen in which these folks can hide out. Recently, we were in a computer store purchasing software and were absolutely blown away by both the quantity and the variety of software and hardware gadgets, games, and joysticks—all the tools used by media-bators to escape life into the un-life of perpetual cyberdistraction.

Most of us have descended into the un-life at one time or another. The good news is that you don't need to call a doctor or go to a miracle crusade to be healed from the un-life. If the four Ds describe you, then the way to a passionate, fulfilling life is through the antidote of the four Gs: You must become *grounded*, *grouped*, *giving*, and *growing*.

How to Get a Life

1. Get Grounded

Getting grounded is the foundation for getting a life. It is all about having a solid identity and sense of self. This includes everything from recognizing one's worth and value to feeling confident and secure. Individuals with a solid identity can't be shaken or devastated just because they don't have a boyfriend or girlfriend. They know who they are and don't need another human to make them feel complete.

The dominant view in our society is that human worth, value, and happiness are obtained through tangible achievement and performance. In other words, if you have money, popularity, prestige, good looks, and intelligence, *then* you have worth. The message is, "The more you have, the greater your self-esteem." This formula can literally ruin your life.

Judging by this arbitrary standard, entertainment figures, such as Michael Jackson, should be the most centered, self-confident, grounded people on this planet. Michael has talent, money, power, and millions of fans who love and worship him. What a tragedy it has been to watch this "man-child" change his nose, lips, hair, and skin through the years—not to mention the dangerous allegations against him—in an attempt to feel better about himself. In one sense, he has it all, but on the other hand, the King of Pop has nothing. He doesn't know who he is. He is not grounded.

Most of us are not like Michael Jackson. However, we are guilty of going overboard on the externals—our hair, face, body, clothes, possessions, and image—to give us a sense of self-worth. It's like putting a small Band-Aid over a huge wound.

I (Sam) counseled a young lady recently who seemed to have it all: great looks, stylish clothes, tons of friends, and a brand-new car for her eighteenth birthday. Yet she was miserable and lonely. Why? *She had focused on the externals to try to fix the internals.* There is nothing wrong with working out, dressing well, and having people like you, but if you look only to those things to give you a sense of self-worth, you'll *always* be searching.

Self-worth is not something you go out and get. Self-worth is not something you buy, achieve, or obtain. It's something you *already* have. Getting grounded means embracing the fact that you are created in the image of God and have worth and value simply because you were born. This value is unchanging and complete. It's not something you can get more or less of depending on your achievements. Worth, based on being in the image of God, does not fluctuate; it does not change regardless of your personality, performance, or possessions because it's based on the immutable character of God.

> Self-worth is not something you go out and get. . . . It's something you **already** have.

Think of it this way: God Himself made you, and He made you *in His image.* That is to say, we are stamped with His image. We speak of money as coming in different denominations such as a dime, a quarter, a five-dollar bill, or a one-hundred-dollar bill. Each coin or bill has two things: an imprint of an image (like George Washington or Abraham Lincoln) and a specified value. For example, a quarter is stamped with the image of George Washington and is worth twenty-five cents. Much in the same way, you are denominated by God's name, you are stamped with His image, and thus your "coin" is of priceless value. Can you put a price on the value of God Almighty? No way, and since you are stamped with the image of the Priceless One, you also are priceless. That is self-worth. Accepting this is the key to being grounded.

In light of this reality, Dr. Peter Kreeft, in *Knowing the God Who Loves You*, says,

> Accept yourself. Love yourself. Respect yourself. This is good advice properly understood. But why should I accept myself if I don't feel like it? What is the rock-solid, inescapable, objective foundation for my self-love? If it is only my feelings or perceptions or my psychologist's perceptions, then my house of self-esteem is built on sand. When the rains come, my house of self-esteem will fall and it will be a cataclysmic fall. But if my house is based on God's Word, then even when the rains of bad feelings and self-doubt come, my house of self-esteem will stand firm because it is built on the rock of God's unchanging truth, not my ever-shifting feelings about myself. Self-esteem is necessary for all psychological health, and there is no absolutely sure basis for self-esteem other than the assurance of God's love for me.[1]

When you see yourself the way God sees you, you will be free from insecurity and fear. What you believe about yourself and your core identity determines how you behave. Getting grounded is ultimately about being established in the rock-solid reality of God's love and favor to you.

2. Get Grouped

Psychologists say that one of our deepest needs is to be connected with others in a meaningful way. You were created by God with the desire to be in relationships with other people, and when this God-given desire goes unmet, you will suffer. You will experience an emptiness and longing that can only be filled when you are associated with others. *Getting grouped is all about developing healthy relationships.* It is being involved with others beyond superficiality. It is about being in deeper relationships where there is trust, safety, and vulnerability.

The TV series *Friends* was one of the top-rated TV shows in America for nearly a decade. Its success was partially due to its emphasis on relationships and getting grouped. The characters on the show—Monica, Chandler, Ross, Phoebe, Rachel, and Joey—are all singles living in New York City. These characters form a type of family, giving each other support and encouragement (in a backhanded sort of way) as they face life's daily struggles.

In our experience, we don't think it is a coincidence that the guys and girls who are passionate about life, God, and making a difference in the world are always involved in some sort of group. It may be a service group, Bible study, or some sort of sports team, but the bottom line is that they are connected with others on a deep level. You are not an island or a Lone Ranger. You were designed to be with others!

Are you committed to a local church? Are you part of an accountability group or support group? Are you a member of a sports team? Do you participate in community service projects? Do you have people in your life who encourage you and, when necessary, graciously confront you? Do you have friends who listen to each other and can, over time, reveal their deepest concerns? If not, take this step today. Get plugged in with people in your church, school, or community, and this will help propel you out of the un-life into having a vibrant life.

> You were created by God with the desire to be in relationships with other people, and when this God-given desire goes unmet, you will suffer.

3. Get Giving

Most people who are depressed, detached, or desperate usually don't even consider this next big G of giving. Think about it—when you're feeling this way, your tendency is to focus only on your own needs and wants. In this day and age of self-indulgence, it seems radical, if not heretical, to tell people to focus on someone other than themselves. *The truth is, the key to a life of misery and loneliness is seeking only to please yourself.*

Giving is about meeting the needs of others on a practical level. Do you ask, "What can I give to this friendship?" and not just, "What can I get from it?" People who are grounded and grouped are also seeking to serve and meet the needs of others.

Remember the Dr. Seuss special "How the Grinch Stole Christmas"? The Grinch was that slimy green character who kind of resembles Gollum from Peter Jackson's *Lord of the Rings* (by J.R.R. Tolkien). He was born with a heart three times smaller than normal people, so he was full of anger, jealousy, and envy. But even after he stole Christmas from the Whos in Whoville, he continued to notice their joy and happiness. They kept their contentment because they gave to one another. This so touched the callous old Grinch that he turned around and started giving Christmas back to the Whos. When he did this, his heart grew three times in size.[2]

Do you want your heart to shrink or to grow? Get outside of yourself, and start giving to others around you. You will be amazed how your own life will be enriched in the process. Speaking of growing, that brings us to the fourth and final G of getting a life.

4. Get Growing

In all aspects of life, things can be stagnant or growing. If you are not growing, expanding, or improving your life, you may be stagnant. Now you would think that almost everyone wants to be fully alive and passionate about life, but some people are little more than walking corpses because they have *stopped* growing. Growing requires the willingness to learn, improve, explore, discover, and sometimes to reach out and "boldly go where you haven't gone before."

How do you grow? It's simple. Ask yourself, "What do I have a passion for?" or "What are my skills and gifts? What am I interested in doing with my life?" For many of you, this is no problem because you are already involved in various extracurricular activities that meet this requirement. However, if you are not, then plug in to some endeavor: art, drama, music, sports, dance, or something else that you are interested in. Certainly, one of your most important areas for growth involves spiritual maturity—study, prayer, and church group affiliation for starters.

You may be thinking, *Wow. This sounds risky. What if I fail?* So what? Even failure is a learning, growing experience. *Success comes from good judgment, good judgment comes from experience, and experience comes from making mistakes.* The key to growing is risk. Leo Buscaglia once said, "The person who risks nothing, does nothing, has nothing, and is nothing. To laugh is to risk being a fool. To weep is to appear sentimental. To reach out to others is to risk getting involved. To love is to risk not being loved in return. The person who risks nothing may avoid suffering and sorrow but he simply cannot know, feel, change, grow, live, or love."[3]

Take a risk and start something new—join a sports team or a band, get a hobby, and throw yourself into life. Seize the day. Dare to lead an extraordinary life.

Consequences of Breaking
This Commandment

- You will be bored, depressed, lonely, self-centered, worried, and hopeless. And it just keeps getting worse because the longer you live the un-life, the more ill you become. Sounds pretty bad, doesn't it?

- Just in case you haven't gotten the picture, let's sum up the consequences with one final question: Would you want to hang out with a lazy, unhappy, lonely, self-obsessed, withdrawn couch potato? Of course not! That's why you must follow this commandment. If you choose not to obey, then just expect to continue repelling everyone and being unhappy.

Benefits of Keeping
This Commandment

- When you have a life of your own, you are attractive to others (and we don't mean just the opposite sex!). That's the first benefit of getting a life. People who exude confidence, stability, and a passion for living inevitably draw others to themselves like a magnet. This is simply a natural by-product of this first law.

- By focusing on getting a life now, you will greatly increase the odds of having healthy and rewarding relationships when you begin dating more seriously in a few years. Your capacity for intimacy will be enhanced, and your ability to handle the challenges that come with relationships will be strengthened. You will be more interesting to people because you'll have something to offer that may enlighten and inform others.

- You will not have unhealthy expectations for a boyfriend or girlfriend to meet your emotional needs and complete you. You will be confident in who you are as an intelligent, independent person with lots of value.
- Ultimately, you will be content, happy, and have an inner peace. This joy will spring from you because you are passionate about life. You know who you are, you have a support system, you have direction, and you are seeking to serve others.

Help for You Who Have Broken This Commandment

- Relax. A mistake or two isn't the end of the world but an opportunity for change. Let this motivate you to find a real existence. Let the symptoms of the un-life serve as a catalyst for change.
- Review the four Gs of getting a life, and take action today. Don't overanalyze the situation and paralyze yourself. Begin to take deliberate, intentional steps to pursue a life. Peace, happiness, purpose, and a passion for living will follow those who follow this commandment. You can do it. So get grounded, get grouped, get giving, and get growing. You'll be glad you did!

Still Don't Believe Us? Check This Out:

- "I [Jesus] came to give life—life in all its fullness" (John 10:10).
- "The thing you should want most is God's kingdom and doing what God wants. Then all these other things you need will be given to you" (Matt. 6:33).
- "Your heart will be where your treasure is" (Matt. 6:21).

Thou Shalt Use Your Brain

Michelle and Josh were infatuated. They couldn't get enough of each other. They had found their respective soul mates and the fulfillment of their wildest dreams. They were "in love." *But everyone else knew better.* Friends and family all insisted that these two didn't belong together. Michelle and Josh were way too serious and had little in common. They had only known each other for two months, and yet they acted as if they were engaged and were going to spend the rest of their lives together.

Sound familiar? Have you ever found yourself saying, "Why does she stay with that jerk?" Or, "Can't he see what a ditz she is?" Most of us have experienced the frustration of watching someone we care about drop his or her friends and get involved in a relationship that is too serious or just doesn't make sense. Worse yet, maybe you have found yourself in the midst of a relationship driven by nothing but raw emotion, and you later wish you'd never met that person. How do you account for this bizarre activity? What is responsible for such behavior? The culprit is *romantic love.*

In this chapter we will help you distinguish between *romantic* love and *real* love. We will also tell you about three major forces of romantic love and how some people get sucked into the Romance Vortex. Then we will demonstrate how you can avoid the pitfalls of Hollywoodized "true romance" by using your brain. *The key is using your head in matters of the heart.* Remember, your brain is located above the neck, not in the chest cavity or below your belt.

> **Remember, your brain is located above the neck, not in the chest cavity or below your belt.**

The Grand Illusion

Ah, the ecstasy of romantic love. Nothing beats that magical experience of locking eyes with the guy or girl of your dreams across a crowded room, falling head over heels in love, and spending every waking moment with that person. If you're not yet familiar with how this thing works, you don't have to look far to see what we're talking about. In cutesy television sitcoms and weepy Hollywood movies, the prince falls in love with the princess, they get married, and everyone lives happily ever after. It all sounds great.

There's only one small problem—this is an illusion. This doesn't happen in real life. Never has. Never will. What we are saying is that *romantic love has little to do with real love.*

Let's face it, as a society we are confused about love. We are constantly inundated with messages about love from music, movies, and other media to the extent that our understanding of true love has been severely distorted. We are easily fooled into thinking that love is just a feeling. As one person put it,

"It's feeling that feeling that we have never felt with anyone else." Although deep down we all want to believe the fairy-tale version of love, sooner or later we must face the truth. Real love doesn't just "happen" to you. Love is not simply a feeling; it is much more.

What is real love? This is one of the great questions of life, and for centuries philosophers have tried and tried to define love. Looking back, we can see that some of the ancient definitions of real love far surpass the recent silliness that pop culture often depicts. The Greek culture was one step ahead of us when it came to defining love. They were not content to talk of love in such general and vague terms as we use today. For example, they made clear distinctions between *eros* (romantic love) and *agape* (real or mature love).

According to the Greeks, *eros* is the passionate form of love. It includes all the elements of that initial "feel-good" phase of a relationship: obsession, mystery, fun, excitement, and passion. *Eros* is driven by emotion. On the other hand, *agape* is the kind of love that two people who deeply care and are concerned about the welfare of the other demonstrate. *Agape* is a mature and stable kind of love—solid, enduring, and providing a sense of security.

> **Romantic love has little to do with real love.**

It is best to consider romantic love and real love as two separate and distinct conditions. Real love is a decision to seek the good of another, whatever the cost. *Agape* includes nurture, support, encouragement, acceptance, and companionship. When it comes to crafting a lasting relationship, whether it be a friendship or possibly a marriage on down the road, real love far outlasts the fleeting emotions of *eros*. *Eros* is not designed to bear the weight of life's stresses. People who base their relationships only on how they *feel* rarely see such relationships last. Friends will inevitably let you down some of the time. But if you have taken the time to allow *agape* to flourish, a solid foundation of loyalty, acceptance, and trust will carry you through those tough times.

Value in Romance?

So what does all this mean for you? Well, we understand that romantic feelings are normal and natural, but, given this stage in your life, they must be kept in perspective. You are too young to be engaged in serious dating, and, quite frankly, you should only think of romance as a fleeting feeling that shouldn't be taken too seriously. We like to think of it as a temporary glue that gives you time to get to know others—to hang out with them and see what they're made of. And, in turn, it's an opportunity for you to learn how to relate to the opposite sex and develop your own relationship skills. Unfortunately, most people do not take advantage of this valuable growth opportunity, and they merrily roll along the waves of passion all the way into serious mistakes. You must make a commitment up front to balance romance with common sense, reason, judgment, and discernment. Remember, the key is to use your head in matters of the heart.

Three Drives of Romantic Love

We believe that romantic love consists of three very powerful drives that can interfere with our ability to use the brain: *emotions*, *hormones*, and *"spiritual"* vibes. Any of these drives by themselves or in combination can cause you to become disoriented, delusional, and even drop one hundred IQ points in a matter of seconds. What happens when you allow these drives to dictate your relationships? We will look at the following real-life love stories and the results of disobeying the commandment to use your brain. As you will see, the consequences can be tragic and far-reaching.

1. Emotion-Driven Dating

Brent met Kelly by "divine fate" at a friend's graduation party. They immediately fell head over heels in love and became consumed with each other day and night. She felt that she had found the missing piece to her life in him because he made her feel so complete. Likewise, he felt she was the one because she made him feel so alive. No one had ever made them feel *that* way. It was a feeling that can only be described as "out of this world." Gazing into each other's eyes, they promised themselves to each other.

Here it gets really scary. They graduated from high school and, during a fast-track engagement, parents and friends asked them the following questions: "Don't you think you should wait a while before getting married?" "What do you think about his/her family?" "What are your future plans after high school?" They chirped back, "It doesn't matter. Everything will work out because we're in love." They couldn't have cared less about the details—they were content to trust their emotions on this one. Everyone tried to reason with them. Their parents even tried to make a last-ditch effort, forbidding the marriage, but Brent and Kelly wouldn't listen. A year later they became a part of the 200,000 people annually who divorce before their two-year anniversary! If only they had slowed down long enough to use their brains! Sadly, they bought into the lie that romantic feelings equal love and that those feelings last forever. Relationships built on emotionalism can be deadly.

2. Hormone-Driven Dating

Nothing interferes with dating and common sense more than the sex drive. For years we have referred to this as the Brain Relocation Phenomenon, which occurs when you are passionate about someone and you start to get physically involved as a way to express that passion. Here's how it works: once the hormones kick in, the brain dislodges from the skull and slowly moves down the body, through the neck, shoulders, chest, stomach, and, finally, below the waist. This process takes ten to twenty minutes for women and about three seconds for men. But once it happens, it's too late! You are thinking and reasoning with your hormones instead of your brain.

> **Nothing interferes with dating and common sense more than the sex drive.**

A typical scenario is that of Abbey and Daniel. They started out group dating, going places with their friends and seeing each other a lot but always with other people around. Gradually they began to spend time alone, going to her house after school before her parents came home, or parking his car in a secluded place just to "talk." And before long—you guessed it—they were having sex. Despite their attempts at "responsible" sex (as if there is such a thing outside of marriage), Abbey got pregnant. Now, rather than going away to her dream school, Abbey attends the local community college during the evenings while her parents keep the baby. Daniel sees the baby on weekends. In this all-too-common scenario, five lives are now experiencing the repercussions of Abbey and Daniel's selfish, brainless behavior.

3. "Spirit"-Driven Dating

There is nothing quite as dangerous as the "oh-so-religious" people who spiritualize their dating processes. Countless guys and girls are listening to what they perceive as the "voice on high" instead of listening to common sense. Actually, this is *not* being spiritual at all because true spirituality is healthy.

"Spirit"-driven dating is pseudospiritual. The following story says it all.

Jason and Karen met each other at a youth camp, and after one of those kum-ba-yah bonfire experiences, Jason just knew God wanted him to date Karen. After all, she was a Christian, and they could study the Bible and spend time together in prayer. In his emotional excitement, Jason told Karen of his "divine" revelations as they walked back to their cabins. Karen was absolutely thrilled. *What a spiritual guy,* she thought. *This is the kind of boyfriend I've always wanted.*

After camp, they started meeting together to read the Bible and pray. Each week they sat a little closer, held hands while they talked, and, before long, the reading and prayer was just an excuse to spend time together. With all of this intimate alone time, they became physically involved. After weeks of continuing this, Karen felt more and more guilt and finally had the courage to break up with Jason. Their "spirit-led" romance ended in a yucky, disillusioning breakup.

If you depend solely on so-called spiritual leadings and fail to use your brain, you could easily end up in a similar situation. We have seen too many teenagers start to date someone just because "that person is a Christian, so it must be God's will" for them. They start spending a lot of time alone to do "spiritual" things, and, inevitably, they end up doing very *unspiritual* things. Without question, this is one of the most common misuses of spirituality. Believe us, at your age, with all those hormones raging inside of you, your prayer and Bible study partners should always be with people of your same gender.

Does that mean we are opposed to guys and girls looking at the Bible and having spiritual conversations together? No way! In fact, we believe it's great for you to have Christian friends of both sexes who will encourage you in your walk with God. The important point is to have those regular, deep conversations and times of prayer with friends of the same sex. It'll save you a lot of unnecessary temptation and confusion. Just remember, God gave us our minds for a reason, and using common sense is indispensable when making godly decisions.

Do you see what happens to people when they allow themselves to be guided by emotions, sexual passion, or "heavenly" voices? Hearts are broken, dreams are dashed, unplanned children get stuck in the middle. This does not have to be your life story. You can make a commitment now to use your brain throughout the dating process.

A Brain Is a Terrible Thing to Waste

We have identified five steps you can take to help promote maximum brain usage.

1. **B**alance the head and the heart.
2. **R**efrain from physical intimacy.
3. **A**void serious dating.
4. **I**nclude others in the process.
5. **N**ever neglect opportunities to evaluate along the way.

If you can make a commitment to implement these five steps, you will be well on your way to using your brain and not just your emotions, hormones, and "spirituality."

1. Balance the Head and the Heart

We are not antiromance, antipassion, or antiprayer. You may be tired of that disclaimer by now, but we do not want to be misunderstood. The simple truth is, somewhere in the process of looking at the opposite sex, you've got to push those big three aside and use your head. I (Ben) remember a particular dating relationship when I literally sat down one evening, pulled out a sheet of paper, and began to list all the pros and cons of the relationship. Then I listed how we benefited each other through our relationship and how we hurt each other through our relationship. Sure, I could have let myself get caught up in the romance, but I had made a conscious decision beforehand that I wouldn't be led by my feelings. Just as eating a balanced diet and living a balanced life will have a positive effect on everything you do, so will balancing the heart and the head in relationships with the opposite sex.

2. Refrain from Physical Intimacy

If you have not been sexually active in the past, this may sound crazy to you (if you have, then you already know), but get this: we are convinced that there is a direct, negative correlation between the intensity of physical contact and the ability to use your brain. That's right. As you increase the physical contact, you lose your ability to reason. How do you refrain from getting too intimate physically?

> **There is a direct, negative correlation between the intensity of physical contact and the ability to use your brain.**

Plan ahead of time to postpone it. This is not about setting some legalistic law or expressing some magical formula, but instead the goal is to avoid having a lot of regrets. Face it, in all likelihood there is a 99.5 percent chance that you are not going to marry any of the people you hang out with right now, so why mess things up by getting physical? You have plenty of time. Save it for later by sticking to these firm lines.

Don't get caught up in holding hands, kissing, or hugging with the opposite sex. Really? *Really.* The longer you refrain from physical contact now, the more special it will be when it actually happens with the right person . . . later. And once you do start dating more exclusively in a few years, start off *slowly*. Don't hold hands, kiss, or hug on the first date—or the second, third, or fourth. This will allow you to build solid friendships without all the confusion and possible regret of having shared too much physical affection. Once you start getting too physically affectionate, the friendship side of your relationship will eventually fall apart. All you think about is getting your hands on each other, and you no longer bother to emphasize the emotional connection.

John and Melanie are both committed Christians, but when they began dropping their friends at the end of their senior year to date more exclusively, they experienced the typical Brain Relocation Phenomenon. Rather than using their heads, John and Melanie plunged ahead, arms around each other and kissing like mad. Within a few weeks, they were far down the road in the physical area, dealing with a hurried cycle of passion, guilt, repentance, and passion again. Although they continued to date after they left for separate colleges, the stresses of a long-distance relationship ultimately did what the dating period did not: reveal how incompatible they were when their brains returned to their normal spots. A bitter breakup ensued.

3. Avoid Serious Dating

When it comes to making bad decisions, nothing will protect you more than avoiding an exclusive, serious dating relationship. You may see your peers pairing off two by two, as though they must find their soul mate before high-school graduation, but stand firm and be patient! You've got plenty of time. In a few years you may begin dating more seriously, but for right now your best bet for happiness and success in future relationships is to avoid serious, exclusive dating.

4. Include Others in the Process

Robert could have saved himself months of heartache and misery if he had only listened to his family and closest friends. When he turned eighteen, he became involved in a dead-end relationship with a young lady. They had little in common and fought over the most trivial things. She tried to control his every move. And, most importantly, they didn't really even like being together. But Robert just kept trying to make it work. Early on, his friends told him to get out of it, but he didn't listen.

Finally, after weeks of not doing anything with his friends, they confronted him about how much time he was spending with her and how she controlled him. They were direct and to the point: he had no life outside of her. This "intervention" session served as a catalyst for Robert to come to his senses and end the relationship.

It's essential to get feedback from a friend, mentor, or family member. When you're interested in someone, it's easy to get so wrapped up in the emotions of being in love and feeling wonderful that you ignore red flags. In fact, we suggest that you have at least two people who hold you accountable for your relationships with the opposite sex—how much you're seeing him or her and what you do when you're together. Robert hung on to a relationship that should have lasted a month at the most, but he simply refused to listen to others' counsel. He wasted a lot of time, energy, and money because he didn't include other people in the evaluation process.

If you have a life and you are in a group with solid, trusted friends, then it should be natural to involve them in the process. Don't ignore their input. Listen to them and weigh their advice. Trust me, it can save you from a heap of pain and misery. We have heard people moan and groan after a breakup: "If only I had listened to my roommate." "If only I had listened to my parents." You do not have to live in the "If only's" of Regret World. Include others in the process of your dating life, and you won't regret the decisions you make.

5. Never Neglect Opportunities to Evaluate Along the Way

One of the most neglected parts of a relationship is evaluation. Once you include others in the process of analysis, you'll have time to think about their words of caution or affirmation and compare them to what you believe is true. Because many people allow their hormones, emotions, or "mystic intuitions" to be their guides, they rarely take time out to sit down in a sober moment and simply think about what's going on. Granted, you may feel it will spoil the thrill of being in love if you start to analyze too much, and that's partly true. You don't want to develop "analysis paralysis," but you still need to take time to evaluate. Eventually we all get over the infatuation phase of the relationship. You know this phase—you are smiling ear to ear, but you are totally blind to each other's shortcomings. Once you move past this period, which usually can last anywhere from nine days to nine months, depending on how long your denial capabilities are functioning, ask yourself these pertinent questions:

> **Just as you might take a car in for a routine maintenance inspection, do the same for your relationships with the opposite sex.**

- Do I enjoy this person as a friend?
- Is there mutual giving and sharing?
- Is there any aspect of his or her personality that I can't tolerate?
- Do I feel encouraged, affirmed, and challenged by this person?
- In what ways do we benefit each other?

- In what ways do we hurt each other?

- Does he or she have a bad temper or act out anger in an abusive manner? (See Chapter 8, "Thou Shalt Not Ignore Warning Signs.")

- Are we spending too much time alone?

Use these questions and others along the way to give yourself a relationship inspection. Just as you might take a car in for a routine maintenance inspection, do the same for your relationships with the opposite sex. It may be a pain to do, but boy, is it even more painful and expensive if you don't.

Do you see the importance of using your brain? Go with the feelings flow, and pain awaits you. Use your brain, and you will avoid heartache and regrets that can follow you around for years. Appreciate the gooeyness of romantic love for what it is, but don't let it run away with you—engage your brain. Don't rush this dating thing. After all, you've got plenty of time.

Consequences of Breaking This Commandment

- You will feel disillusioned and cheated when you wake up one day and realize what a moron you've been hanging with.

- You will feel let down by God because you feel that He "led" you into this relationship.

- You will feel embarrassed, ashamed, and foolish because you didn't see what was going on in the beginning.

- You will have wasted time, energy, emotion, and money on someone you should have seen right through from the beginning.

Benefits of Keeping
This Commandment

- You will be learning the valuable art of wise love choices, something you will fall back on for a long time.

- You will more readily be able to discern dead-end, loser relationships.

- You will avoid having a lot of regrets later.

- You will be able to distinguish important inner qualities in people from less important physical and personality traits.

Help for You Who Have Broken
This Commandment

- Admit that you are an emotional, hormonal, and "spiritual" junkie. (Come on, admit it. We've all been there.)

- Now make the commitment to use your head in matters of the heart.

- Determine to apply the BRAIN acrostic to balance the head and the heart, refrain from physical intimacy, avoid serious dating, include others in the process, and never neglect opportunities to evaluate along the way.

Still Don't Believe Us?
Check This Out:

- "Listen carefully to wisdom; set your mind on understanding. Cry out for wisdom, and beg for understanding. Search for it like silver, and hunt for it like hidden treasure. . . . Good sense will protect you; understanding will guard you" (Prov. 2:2–4, 11).

- "He who trusts in his own heart is a fool, But whoever walks wisely will be delivered" (Prov. 28:26 NKJV).

- "Trust the LORD with all your heart, and don't depend on your own understanding. Remember the LORD in all you do, and he will give you success" (Prov. 3:5–6).

Commandment 3

Thou Shalt Be Equally Yoked

I n the 1978 movie *Grease*, Danny Zuko (John Travolta), a rebellious kid from the wrong side of the tracks, falls in love with Sandy (Olivia Newton-John), a beautiful, blue-eyed blonde with a squeaky-clean image. He's from the poor side of town, and she's from the upper end. He's a leather-jacket-wearing gang member who dates loose women, and she's a preppy cheerleader who dates the quarterback of the football team. He's a street-smart punk, and she's Miss Goody Two-Shoes. These two have virtually nothing in common aside from their sizzling-hot attraction to one another. Essentially, they fall in love and make a few compromises in each other's direction. She puts on a black leather jacket, and he joins the track team. They reunite at the end-of-school carnival, and the entire cast breaks out into dancing, singing, and generally having a good ol' time, while the unlikely duo drives off arm in arm into the sunset.

The "opposites attract" relationship works great on the big screen, but in reality it's extremely difficult to pull off. While it is true that opposites do attract sometimes, the healthiest relationships are those in which the similarities far outweigh the differences. This truth applies not only to dating relationships but to close friendships as well.

In counseling and working with a multitude of couples, we have discovered that there are certain types of relationships that are doomed from the start. We call these Unequally Yoked Relationships (UYRs). This chapter will expose four of the most common UYRs and then show you what to look for in order to establish Equally Yoked Relationships (EYRs).

Unequally Yoked Relationships

There is a passage in the Bible that exhorts Christians not to be yoked with non-Christians. A yoke was a strong wooden bar that was placed around the necks of oxen. This bar was then connected to a plow. The trick was to yoke together two oxen of equal strength so they could move forward to plow a field in a straight line. Unequally yoked oxen would simply move around in circles because they were incompatible. The Bible uses this metaphor to warn believers of the dangers of being "yoked" together with unbelievers—two people who are ultimately headed in opposite directions. In a similar fashion, we aim to warn you of the dangers of dating someone with vast differences. The following is a summary of four unequally yoked relationships.

1. The Missionary Relationship

Jennifer was involved in the youth group at her church. She was junior class president and an honor student as well. One Sunday her youth pastor was talking about the importance of viewing her school as a mission field. In hasty conviction to begin reaching her non-Christian peers, Jennifer dropped her Christian friends and started hanging out with everyone she could find outside her faith. Pretty soon, she began dating a non-Christian guy whom she hoped to eventually convert to her faith and save from his "sinful" lifestyle. Though Jennifer's intentions were good in hanging out with non-Christians, she cratered without the support of her Christian friends and started doing what her new friends, particularly her new boyfriend, were doing.

Jennifer is a "missionary" dater because she rationalized the need to stay in that relationship in order to bring the other person to her faith. Her focus was to get this person to jump through religious hoops and buy into her belief system. Girls are especially vulnerable to this kind of relationship because guys will do anything (yes, anything!) to impress a girl. If a guy needs to walk an aisle, get baptized, speak in tongues, bark, laugh, or even lick the lint out of Buddha's belly button, he'll do it just to keep the girl. Many of you are wondering, "Are all guys that conniving and deceptive?" The answer is *yes*. Furthermore, when emotions and hormones enter the picture, all the rules change. A sincere young woman who simply wants to win a young man to Christ may find herself emotionally attached and find it very difficult to remove herself from this relationship.

Missionary relationships come in all shapes and sizes. However, *the common denominator is the need to justify the relationship on evangelistic grounds*. The "logic" behind this approach disturbs us. For starters, how crazy to think that you can establish a healthy relationship with someone on the basis of a hidden agenda! Does it strike you as slightly dishonest and unfair to deceive another person like this? Unsurprisingly, after you've hung on to these dead-end relationships, it's even more difficult for you to break it off in the end. The bottom line is that when there is spiritual or religious incompatibility, you need to get out. It's too difficult to judge the sincerity of one's spiritual quest when the emotions of love and romance are involved. Missionary relationships simply don't work.

2. The Mother Teresa Relationship

Mother Teresa was one of the most respected and saintly women of all time. Her mission statement was simple: love and comfort the sick and dying in the streets of Calcutta, India. She was annually listed as one of the most admired women of the world. Tragically, some women have adopted this mission statement for their relationships with the opposite sex. They attach themselves to guys who are losers and who care only about themselves. Against all odds, they attempt to love, comfort, and take care of that guy in an effort to help him out. This is what we call a "Mother Teresa relationship": a well-meaning person plays mommy to someone who needs to grow up and get a life.

Lori is a classic case of someone who got into a Mother Teresa relationship. Lori had a crush on a cute basketball player who never gave her the time of day. When she saw he was struggling in their senior physics class, she offered to help him with his homework and preparation for tests. Desperate to pass the class, Brian agreed to study with her. And thus began a strange relationship in which Brian would be nice to Lori when they studied together, but ignore her when they were around other people. Lori kept meeting with him, thinking he would eventually start to like her and appreciate what she was doing for him. He never did. Lori finally told Brian he could do his own work, but only after months of being taken advantage of and used.

We could cite case after case of individuals who have wasted time and energy on someone they thought they could rescue from failing in

> You are called to be an equal partner in a relationship—not a shrink, surrogate parent, missionary, or nurse.

school, getting in trouble with authorities, or worse yet, a drug addiction, alcoholism, or sex addiction. After being warned of the dangers of this kind of relationship, one misguided Mother Teresa–type said, "I have enough love for both of us."

If you have a tendency to attract and hang on to needy people in order to "love" them out of a situation, then you need to ask yourself why. Why are you drawn to these types? Why do you have this unquenchable need to be needed? Why do you think you have the ability to change this person? You are called to be an equal partner in a relationship—not a shrink, surrogate parent, missionary, or nurse. Mother Teresa relationships may seem exciting and challenging at first, but after all the futile attempts to rehabilitate a sick person, they usually end in great disappointment and disillusionment. If this describes you, we suggest you refer back to the first commandment and get grounded. Find your security and stability in God through a relationship with Christ.

3. The Sugar Daddy Relationship

The hallmark of the Sugar Daddy relationship is the substantial age difference between the guy and girl. If you find yourself saying, "Yes sir," to your boyfriend, then you may be in a Sugar Daddy relationship. If he's in college and you're still in high school, then you may be in a Sugar Daddy relationship. If you're planning for your senior prom while he's planning for med school, then you may be in a Sugar Daddy relationship. This type of relationship is usually made up of individuals who are attempting to compensate for unmet emotional needs. One person may be dating someone older just so her friends will think she's cool. The other may be dating someone younger because he isn't mature enough to relate to people his own age, and he can easily impress someone younger. Expecting an older boyfriend or girlfriend to somehow fill in for Dad or Mom represents an unequally yoked relationship. Frankly, there are just too many barriers to overcome in this kind of relationship: you're at different places in life, you have different peers, and you are pursuing different goals. And, more important, this type of relationship can often be extremely dangerous for girls. An older guy who is naturally more experienced in life and love may find a younger girl's naïveté attractive because she is more likely to go along with whatever he wants for the relationship (and sometimes that's just one thing!).

4. The Eminem Relationship

Like it or not, rap superstar Eminem has become a cultural icon and antihero to many teenagers around the world. Eminem is famous—or infamous, depending on your perspective—for his controversial song lyrics on everything from his unpleasant childhood to mainstream media. Though outspoken with his opinion of other musical artists and his stand on certain social issues, he is in reality a rebel whose only "cause" is himself.

Perhaps you haven't been "booed" at the MTV Music Awards or written songs about an abusive childhood, but you still may be in an Eminem relationship. The essence of this kind of relationship is the need to date someone purely out of rebellion. Guys and girls seeking Eminem relationships choose to hang out with people who are exactly the opposite of everything their families would want for them. Let's say you are being raised in a conservative, traditional, Christian home where there is a strong emphasis on attending church and "keeping up appearances." However, if you generally find yourself going out with people who are atheistic, liberal, and antiestablishment, you probably have Eminem relationships.

Anna's upper-middle-class family had a very reputable name in the community. As the youngest child of six, Anna was constantly pampered by her parents, but they never allowed her to make her own decisions or do things on her own. Not surprisingly, a few weeks after graduating from high school, she wound up in an Eminem relationship. She started dating a guy from a different country who had a criminal record. This infuriated her parents and bewildered her closest friends who counseled her otherwise, but she would not listen.

Relationships like Anna's are not uncommon. Most of the

time, people like this are not in love with the person they're seeing, but are merely angry with their parents or are attempting to establish a sense of autonomy and independence. We believe there are more constructive ways to deal with anger or establish independence than taking a walk on the Eminem side. Take it from Eminem's ex-wife and save yourself a lot of heartache, pain, and embarrassment by staying clear of any kind of Eminem relationship.

A whole book could be devoted to Unequally Yoked Relationships that are doomed to fail. We think you get the gist, so let's move on to the Equally Yoked Relationships because these are the relationships that work.

The Equally Yoked Relationship

A relationship, by definition, is the connecting of persons. Therefore, to have a successful close friendship with the same or opposite sex, you must connect on many levels. This is what we call an EYR: Equally Yoked Relationship. Undoubtedly, you have been in relationships where there was a partial connection—you connect on one or two levels, but you sense that something is missing. To truly connect with another person, you must be more than just attracted to each other; you must connect on *spiritual* and *social* levels as well.

The Spiritual Connection

If you cannot connect with someone on a spiritual level, your relationship is headed for disaster. What you believe about God, how you pray, where you worship, the holidays you celebrate, the books you hold to be sacred, and your opinion on baptism are just a few components that make up your spiritual belief system. Your spirituality and how that is expressed is the most intense and intimate part of you.

From a Christian perspective, you should date only Christians. There is no exception. Everyone thinks, *But my*

39

relationship is different. Trust us, it is not. Or they say, "But we're just dating. It's not like I'm going to marry this person." Remember, you will eventually marry someone you date—you might as well start making good decisions now. (Not to mention the fact that your chief purpose for dating at this point is to establish *healthy* patterns of relating to the opposite sex.) Remember: a non-Christian may have a very different agenda!

> You will eventually marry someone you date—you might as well start making good decisions now.

If you could just listen to the tales of relational carnage that we hear from married couples trying to keep it together as they vehemently oppose each other on an issue that stems from their deeply held religious convictions, you would avoid such a dating relationship. Choose wisely, starting *now*!

Many Christians fall into the trap of dating a non-Christian because they never bother asking that person about his or her beliefs. Others simply assume that the person they are dating is a Christian because, after all, "He told me he was a Christian." There is no doubt that only God knows who is a real Christian and who is not, but He does lay down a few guidelines to help you discern if the person you are going out with is a genuine Christian.

Personal testimony. Someone who knows Jesus Christ will be able to point to a certain time in life when he or she personally trusted Him as Lord and Savior. A Christian makes a conscious decision to repent of sin and to trust and follow Christ. A mature believer feels no fear or shame acknowledging and discussing this critical life foundation.

Changed lifestyle. A Christian seeks to live according to the principles set forth in the Bible. Believers attend church and desire to hang out with other Christians. They seek to love others and bring them into a personal relationship with Christ. Christians value sexual purity and don't take advantage of the people they're dating. They desire to study, pray, and apply the Scriptures to their lives. They forgive others because they have received abundant forgiveness from God. Of course, this doesn't mean they are perfect, but there will be a marked difference in their lives.

Be sure that your closest friends, of both sexes, are people you can connect with on a spiritual level. If you are a Christian, be certain that whomever you choose to date has had a "real deal" encounter with Christ and, as a result, has a changed life. You'll be glad you did.

The Social Connection

Some people often ignore or neglect social compatibility, though this very area creates lots of stress for relationships. Social compatibility primarily concerns family patterns and social relating. We'll explain.

Family matters. The old saying "The apple doesn't fall far from the tree" usually holds true. Who you are and many of your perspectives (big and small) on life stem directly from your family upbringing. If you live in a home where you receive love, support, encouragement, and security from your parents, then you probably have a good foundation for building healthy relationships with other people. If you don't live in such an environment, then you will have to work a little harder to develop good relationships.

Following are some of the more important issues associated with family background:

- religious beliefs and practices
- family rules
- parental support (Do their parents give a flip about where they are and what they're doing?)
- work ethic (Do their parents encourage them to work hard and succeed in academics, sports, and other activities?)
- resolving conflict (How does their family treat one another when they disagree?)

Given the incredible influence of one's family life, it remains all too important that you seek to date people you connect with on this level.

The other area of connecting at the social level deals with patterns of relating. This dimension of a relationship covers a wide variety of concerns, including:

- social skills
- level of social involvement
- how to spend free time (i.e., hobbies, interests)
- gravitation toward similar types of people
- communication style
- intellectual compatibility

So what does it mean to be equally yoked in this area? Well, similarities between people make life together much simpler. Friendships, by necessity, involve compromise, and people can reach compromises more easily when they share common values and interests. How can you ever have fun with someone with whom you have nothing in common? If you are a major extrovert who loves being involved in social activities, going to your high-school football games, and playing in a band with your friends, you're probably not going to have a great time with a guy or girl who clams up around people, likes to stay at home on weekends, and hates rock concerts. Being unequally yoked to someone can turn even the smallest of decisions into big problems. Sure, sometimes opposites can attract, but for a stable relationship, bet on similarity.

Consequences of Breaking This Commandment

- You will experience a lot of pain, frustration, and confusion because you are dating someone who is nothing like you.
- You will drive yourself (and the guy or girl you're with) crazy because you are trying to change the unchangeable.

Benefits of Keeping This Commandment

- You'll be able to truly connect and enjoy the company of people who value the same things as you.
- You will be on the same page morally, socially, and mentally with the people you hang out with.
- You will avoid much of the stress and conflict that come with trying to date someone you don't understand and who doesn't understand you.

Help for You Who Have Broken This Commandment

- Relax. If we hadn't broken this commandment several times we couldn't have written this book.

- If you are in a UYR right now, it's time to set some relational boundaries (see Commandment Five), and prepare for God's best for you sometime in the future.

Still Don't Believe Us? Check This Out:

- "You are not the same as those who do not believe. So do not join yourselves to them. Good and bad do not belong together. Light and darkness cannot share together. How can Christ and Belial, the devil, have any agreement? What can a believer have together with a nonbeliever?" (2 Cor. 6:14–15).

- "Do not be deceived: 'Bad company corrupts good morals'" (1 Cor. 15:33 NASB).

- "Spend time with the wise and you will become wise, but the friends of fools will suffer" (Prov. 13:20).

Thou Shalt Take It Slow

Remember when you were a kid and you could hardly wait 'til Christmas? No matter how many times your Sunday school teacher said, "Jesus is the reason for the season," and you tried to be good and ponder that truth, Christmas meant one thing to you then: presents. So, shortly after Thanksgiving the search would begin. You would scour the house, hoping to catch a glimpse of what might be awaiting you Christmas morning. Perhaps you would search closets, underneath beds, even the trunk of your parents' car. Or maybe you were one of those who shook every present under the tree and tried to pull back just a corner of the wrapping paper for a peek that might tell all. When it comes to Christmas, every kid feels the same: "It just can't get here fast enough."

Ever wonder why relationships with the opposite sex feel the same way? Once love is in the air, things just can't move fast enough. You feel as though you need to see this person every waking moment, or at least be on the phone with him or her. He or she is all you think about, all you dream about, all you talk about. If you aren't together, you're miserable, and you make everyone around you miserable too.

What is it about relationships that compels us to rush

things—rush to go out again, rush to hold hands, rush to have that first kiss?

Though we may not know the answer to that age-old question, we do know this: *Take it slow, get to know.* We pound this essential motto into teenagers' heads over and over. Take it slow and get to know. Your relationship is doomed to failure and you are in for a lot of regrets if you ignore this commandment. In this chapter you are going to discover two reasons why it is smart to take it slow and how you can actually go about doing so in your relationships with the opposite sex.

Reasons to Take It Slow

1. You Do Not Get to Know a Person in a Short Period of Time

No matter how many hours you spend on the phone in one week, no matter how many times you see each other in one weekend, no matter how incredibly perfect this person seems after one date, you cannot get to know a person in a short period of time.

Believe me, when it comes to fervent explanations as to why your relationship is different, I've heard it all. For example, (1) I know God has told you this person is in His "will" for you, or (2) you have never felt this way about anyone else, or (3) you have stayed up all night talking, and you know everything there is to know about each other. Yada, yada, yada. Trust me, you still need to take it slow. It's impossible to really get to know someone in such a short period of time.

Let's say you meet someone at school, work, or church that you like a lot at first. There is just something about that person that draws you in—you enjoy his or her company, you have a lot in common, you think you are developing a potential lifelong friend. And then . . . one day you discover some major glitches in that person's character. He is a chronic shoplifter, pathological liar, pothead, cat abuser. Fortunately, if you are obeying

Commandment Four and taking it slow, by the time you discover these things you can run—quickly—and will have lost only a potential friend. Had you rushed into a let-me-spend-every-waking-hour-with-you relationship with this loser, things could have gotten ugly. The point is clear: it takes a long time to get to know what is really going on in someone's life. Discerning a person's character takes time.

Discerning a person's character takes time.

So enjoy this time in your life for what it is—a time to get to know others and to discover how to interact successfully with them. It is a legitimate and important time for you to take the opportunity to grow and develop healthy skills of relating. It's not the time to be rushing headlong into a serious or committed relationship just because you feel great about that special someone. Take it slow!

2. You Protect Yourself from Getting Too Attached Too Quickly

Another reason you should take it slow is that it allows you to guard yourself from getting emotionally attached. A verse in the Bible says, "Do not throw your pearls to pigs" (Matt. 7:6 NIV). Many young people are gifted at tossing their pearls, and there are plenty of pigs who are willing to catch them.

When you have an initial attraction to someone that is so strong you can feel your heart beating through your chest, it's difficult to chill and not to react to that powerful feeling. I know lots of guys and girls who are romantic love junkies. They live for that indescribable, magical spark that happens when two people feel that instant sense of closeness. Many take that feeling and run with it, spending a billion hours together on dates, allowing things to progress way too quickly in the physical area, seeing each other every single day, after school, on the weekends, and on and on. This is a formula for short-term pleasure, long-term pain.

Of course, one day they wake up and realize they are absolutely sick of being with this person. They smothered each other so much that the love flame was extinguished. Others have a worse fate: they never slow down long enough to catch a breath, and the next thing they know, they've got a lot of sexual history with a person they barely even know.

If you take it slow early on, then you won't become a love junkie or wind up with a bunch of regrets. When you seek to take it slow, you limit sharing yourself emotionally and you hold off physical affection until you are ready to enter an exclusive dating relationship one day. This protects you from giving your heart and body to someone you don't really know, and allows you to get out of a relationship without having invested too much emotional and spiritual energy on the wrong person.

The ancient biblical philosopher Solomon said it best when he wrote, "Guard your heart, for it is the wellspring of life" (Prov. 4:23 NIV). Do yourself a favor and take it slow. Guard your heart—don't throw your pearls before pigs. You'll make a lot of friends and save your heart, soul, and body for the right one.

Seven Slow-Motion Dating Strategies

Because of the natural tendency to speed at the beginning of a relationship, you must have a strategy locked in place to help you keep it in low gear. Here is our list of seven strategies that must be employed.

1. Remember your age.
2. Enjoy group dates as much as possible.

3. Make one-on-one dates short and casual.

4. Delay physical affection and keep definite boundaries.

5. Stay connected with your friends.

6. Do not pray together.

7. Don't even think about mentioning the "M" word.

1. Remember Your Age

So you're sick of us reminding you that you're too young for serious dating? Too bad. We'll say it again. You've got years ahead of you before you'll want to give your heart away once and for all, so save your heart (and the rest of you too) for that one down the road. Enjoy casual relationships with the opposite sex and focus on building great friendships.

2. Enjoy Group Dates as Much as Possible

Spending time with that special someone within a group context is one of the most secure methods for taking it slow. Including others provides a natural form of accountability and an appropriate atmosphere of safety. Furthermore, it sets a lighthearted and casual tone that is necessary to minimize the temptation to take yourselves too seriously.

3. Make One-on-One Dates Short and Casual

Assuming you have the green light from your parents to spend time in one-on-one situations, we strongly recommend that you make these times together short and informal. Once again, there is no need to act "serious" or committed, because that just doesn't fit! I (Ben) remember making some of the most ridiculous mistakes of my life when I dated in college. I used to get real intense, asking deep, philosophical questions and staying up half the night trying to solve the world's problems on dates with girls I barely knew. Finally, after "falling in love" countless times, I got a clue and started making my early dates a lot shorter and a whole lot more casual.

When you start off slowly, it's a whole lot easier to continue that process. Go watch your brother's baseball game together, grab some pizza, and then join your friends for a movie. If your parents don't give you a curfew, give yourself one and stick to it! We didn't say it would be easy to have short, casual dates (especially if you *really* like somebody), but you'll be the wiser for it.

Another way to keep it slow in the beginning is to limit the number of times you see a person in a week. If you're seeing that person every day at school *and* after school *and* on weekends, cut out some of the after-school and weekend time. This will serve two purposes. First, it will force you to take it slow and easy so that you don't overdose on each other. Second, you will be more attractive to the person you are seeing because it will show that you are not clingy and that you don't need a relationship to make you happy.

4. Delay Physical Affection and Keep Definite Boundaries

Holding hands, hugging, and kissing should be symbols of a secure relationship, not a means of *gaining* a secure relationship. As we've said before, save it. That kind of stuff should be reserved for more serious dating, when you potentially have an eye on marriage. The minute you bring physical affection into a young dating relationship, things change, expectations increase, and communication shuts down. The art of taking it slow means you are committed to getting to know a person gradually and growing into a mature friendship.

> When you bring touch into your relationship, the stakes increase.

When you bring touch into your relationship, the stakes

increase, and it makes ending the relationship all the more difficult. You've gotten so addicted to the physical stuff that you can't see anything else. So you just keep staying in this dead-end relationship that is built only on the physical.

Girls, especially, need to take a firm stand here and not cave in to a guy's advances. Far too many girls have had the audacity to say to me, "Well, if I don't get physical with him, he'll leave." Fine—let him leave! *If you allow a guy to have his way with you, you will never, ever be respected by him.* (More on this in Chapter 7.)

Ultimately, guys are looking for a **CAR**.

C—Guys are looking for a *challenge.* When you constantly hold hands with him or let him kiss you, then you are no longer in the hunt. In other words, you may think that giving in to his physical advances will make him think more of you, but the truth is, he'll end up thinking less and less of your character. When that happens, his attraction to you will soon disintegrate, and he'll simply move on to someone who presents more of a challenge than you did.

A—Guys are looking for someone they are *attracted* to. Attraction has more to do with your personality and character than how you look. Sure, guys ogle and go wild over *Cosmo* supermodels at an initial glance, but in the long haul they are looking for a best friend, not merely a pretty face.

R—Guys are looking for a girl they can *respect.* When you give in to them in the physical area, you immediately lose their respect.

5. Stay Connected with Your Friends

One of the worst things you can do in the dating process is to ditch your friends the moment you feel like you've met someone special. Maintaining your gender-specific friendships will prevent you from getting sucked into the relational speed zone. When some people fall in love they have a tendency to punt their friends and OD on their new romantic interest. This kind of behavior usually hacks off their friends and scares off the potential romance. Stay connected with your friends. You will definitely need their advice and feedback throughout the dating process. They'll help keep you accountable. Another reason you don't dump your friends: you will need them if and when you dump someone or you get dumped.

6. Do Not Pray Together

The "let's be prayer partners" approach sounds sweet and spiritual on the surface, but it can actually be used as a form of manipulation. Praying is one of the most intimate experiences you can ever have. Consider the fact that when you pray with someone you hardly know, you are encouraging a bond that can be more intense than even physical affection or sex. There is a fine line between spirituality and sexuality, and people who do not respect that line are in danger of getting burned.

Let's say you have an intense attraction to someone you have met at church. He finally asks you out, and you gleefully accept. After pizza and a movie, he takes you back to your house, and you proceed to talk a little while in his car. After a while, you get out of the car, and instead of trying to hug you or kiss you, he says, "Let's pray and thank the Lord for our day." Well, you are absolutely shocked. Not only is he *not* trying to put a move on you, he is taking the spiritual lead by initiating prayer. Here's where it gets dangerous. Once you start to pray together, you are combining two of the most powerful forces on the planet: your spiritual drive and your sex drive. It's so easy for the two to get convoluted and for you to finish the prayer session thinking you heard a divine word from God that this is The One. In fact, all that you really achieved was a spiritualization of the hormones. So, like we said before, keep your same-sex friends as prayer partners for now.

7. Don't Even Think About Mentioning the "M" Word

If you really want to create emotional chaos and unrealistic expectations early in your life, then just mention the "M" word. The "M" word is *marriage*. You may be thinking, *Marriage? At my age? Are you crazy?* But believe us, some teenagers are already thinking that way—just look at all the promise rings that are being given as pre-engagement tokens. Any discussion of marriage will cause the hormones to rage because of this assumption: "This could be The One for life." Most students are able to control the physical aspect of their relationship fairly well until the focus shifts to a future life together.

Deciding whom to marry is one of the biggest decisions you'll ever make, and it is not one to be made at this age. No matter how difficult it may be, no matter how many little coincidences have occurred that prove you are destined to be united, no matter how many divine revelations you receive, and in spite of the comments and hints dropped by overeager and well-meaning friends, hear this: Resist until the end. Wait. Don't talk about marriage until you've had a chance to grow up a little.

Consequences of Breaking This Commandment

- You damage friendships with the people you'll need to have around during and after the relationship.
- You potentially push someone away by smothering him or her and appearing desperate.
- You risk being deceived by someone with impure motives.

Benefits of Keeping This Commandment

- You'll avoid jumping into a relationship with someone you don't really know.

- You'll avoid being manipulated and controlled emotionally, physically, and spiritually.
- You'll avoid the heartache of emotionally or physically bonding with someone too early and scattering yourself.
- You'll experience more enjoyment in seeing a relationship develop gradually, rather than rushing through it.

Help for You Who Have Broken This Commandment

- Put on the brakes in your relationship—it's never too late to slow things down—or even break up.
- Get grouped. Avoid exclusive dating by going out with a group of your friends.
- Stop ditching your friends in order to be alone. Focus on maintaining your friendships.
- Set clear emotional boundaries and physical limits.

Still Don't Believe Us? Check This Out:

- "Whoever loves discipline loves knowledge, but he who hates reproof is stupid" (Prov. 12:1 NASB).
- "Guide my steps as you promised; don't let any sin control me" (Ps. 119:133).
- "I praise the LORD because he advises me. Even at night, I feel his leading. I keep the LORD before me always. Because he is close by my side, I will not be hurt" (Ps. 16:7–8).

Thou Shalt Set Clear Boundaries

He ran over you with his motorcycle?" I exclaimed at the top of my lungs, responding to one of the most outlandish calls I have ever received on the radio. "Yes, that's right," Brooke replied with a soft voice. "But you see, I don't think he meant to. He was just showing off in front of his friends and—," she continued before I interrupted her. "Brooke, do you hear what you're saying? This guy is a maniac who should be behind bars, and you are wondering whether or not you should keep going out with this loser? *The guy tried to kill you! He ran over you with a motorcycle, for crying out loud!* Case closed. Next issue please."

Even though Brooke survived the attempted Harley-Davidson homicide, she went groveling back to this creep and continued having sex with the guy as if nothing had ever happened. To say the least, this young lady was having difficulty setting strong relational boundaries. Now, you may have never been run over by a motorcycle madman, but if you fail to set clear boundaries in your relationships, you will feel as if you have been hit by a Mack truck. If you can relate to any of the following statements, you are struggling with big-time boundary issues:

- "I seem to have the hardest time saying no to people I care about."

- "When she's in a bad mood, I get in a bad mood too. It just ruins my whole day."

- "I've noticed that my boyfriends always take advantage of me. I must be picking the wrong guys."

- "I give so much of my time and effort to a relationship and I never seem to get anything in return!"

The common denominator in all of the situations mentioned above is one of responsibility. If you take too much responsibility for your friends or fail to take enough responsibility for yourself, then you have serious boundary problems. This fifth law of relationships has to do with being able to define yourself and maintain your sense of separateness within a relationship. Setting clear boundaries helps you to know what to take responsibility for, and it helps others know how to relate to you more effectively. If you fail to take responsibility and set boundaries, then watch out because you might get run over.

In this chapter, we will explore what boundaries are. Then we'll look at four areas in which we all must set boundaries and four myths that say drawing lines is wrong. Finally, we will look at the role of boundaries in a breakup.

What Is a Relational Boundary?

Boundaries define who you are, and they reinforce the idea that you are separate and distinct from others. They describe what you think and feel, as well as what you are willing to do. They also define your preferences, what you like and dislike, what you will accept and won't accept. They inform you as to where you end and others begin. Most important, boundaries help you determine what you are and are not responsible for.

All healthy relationships *require* good, solid, and well-defined relational boundaries.

How to Stop People from Running over You

> All healthy relationships require good, solid, and well-defined relational boundaries.

The only way to stop people from running all over you is to let your yes be yes and your no be no. In other words, *boundaries are about drawing lines.* Have you ever made someone so angry that he or she said, "Hey, that's where I draw the line. Enough is enough!" Too many daters don't know how to draw the line, when to draw the line, or where to draw the line. Here are a few areas where you must learn how to draw the line and let your yes be yes and your no be no. Follow these principles, and you will become a healthy Line Drawer—someone who sets appropriate boundaries.

1. Your Body Belongs to You

You must draw definite lines in the physical/sexual area or you will get blitzed in the dating process. We cannot underestimate the importance of clearly defining limits in this area. At the risk of insulting your intelligence, let's begin with the understanding that your body belongs to you. You alone are responsible for your body. We're talking about the ability to define what your limits are before you even step out the door on a Friday night. Physical boundaries include the ability to say no when a person wants to go beyond what you believe is appropriate. If he or she doesn't respect those beliefs (i.e., you find yourself saying, "What part of no don't you understand?"), consider this a *blatant* violation of your boundaries. Tell that person to back off. If he or she has so little respect for you that the response to your boundaries is callous disregard, get rid of that person. Your relationship will get more hellish if you put up with that disrespect.

If you don't set your boundaries before things get too heavy, then it will be difficult to stop that person from running over you. Just look what happened to Kat. When Kat was in high school, she was one of the most popular girls in school. She was the head cheerleader, captain of the swim team, and a member of the National Honor Society. She also had very high moral standards and made a firm commitment to remain sexually pure until she married. She dated many guys in high school and had one steady boyfriend for her entire senior year, but never got too physical. However, when she left home for college she met a guy named Trenton, who started to test her physical boundaries. They began by kissing passionately for hours on end, and then it progressed to foreplay. He told her, "As long as we don't have intercourse, everything else is okay"(a great lie!). After six months they broke up, and Kat felt guilty and ashamed of what she had done with Trenton.

A year later she met another guy at a fraternity party, and she began to do the same things with him that she had done with Trenton. One night, things got intense as they were making out, and she let down her final boundary and had sex with him. Looking back on the event two years later, Kat was in tears because she had given away something that she can never get back.

Like Kat, most people don't lose their boundaries overnight. It's a gradual process of compromise and rationalization, then the next thing you know you are giving your body to someone you're not married to, much less even know very well. In the sexual area you must make the commitment *now* to draw the line. Once you are in the heat of passion, the Brain Relocation

Phenomenon kicks in, and you begin to reason with the wrong parts of your body. God has given you a body, and whether you like your body or not is irrelevant to the issue of being a good steward of it. Respect yourself and the person you are with. We'll talk more about sex in Commandments Six and Seven, but for now, take ownership of your body and remember that it belongs to you.

2. Your Emotions Belong to You

Emotions are strange animals that often seem unpredictable and uncontrollable. However, you and I are still responsible for our emotions and how we express them in our relationships. It sounds silly to state that your emotions "belong to you," but you would be surprised by the number of young people we talk with who don't know where their emotions end and their peers' begin. Some allow their friends to intrude on their lives to an absurd degree. They're basically letting other people control them. Others feel the need to be the intruders and controllers, stepping in and feeling responsible for everything their boyfriend or girlfriend does. The Boundary Police will cite you for a violation either way because *your emotions belong to you (and others' emotions belong to them)*. Thankfully, we have a few fundamentals for setting good emotional boundaries in dating relationships.

First of all, learn to communicate how you feel while still guarding your heart. *The ability and willingness to identify and express what you are truly feeling is probably the single most important factor in promoting healthy relationships.* Simple expressions like, "I feel afraid," "I feel sad," or "I feel lonely," are very powerful statements about you, and they serve to let others know you on a deeper level. Of course, please don't try these statements with people you hardly know (you'll sound silly, at best). In addition, be careful to avoid going too far too fast with your emotions. A couple who on their first date talks for hours on end about their joys, fears, dreams, secrets, and struggles is just too intimate.

> **Be careful to avoid going too far too fast with your emotions.**

Second, you need to own your feelings and be able to separate them from everyone else's. If you discover that your feelings are somehow dictated by a boyfriend's or girlfriend's actions or emotions, then you are too emotionally connected to that person. You are allowing another person to control your emotional state. In short, how he or she is feeling determines whether or not you're going to be in a good mood or a bad mood.

Vince was in love with Zoe, a young lady with a ton of emotional baggage. If Zoe was down in the dumps when Vince saw her, then he would simply adapt his emotions to accommodate her. Throughout their dating, Vince never was able to separate his emotions from Zoe's. He would often waste entire days at school, aimlessly trying to pull Zoe out of her emotional ditch because so-and-so had put her down.

When you find yourself saying things like, "When my girlfriend is sad, it just ruins the entire day," or "When my boyfriend is angry and irritable, I get angry too," you are not drawing the line between yourself and others. No one should have that much control over your emotions. Remember . . . you own your emotions.

Certainly there are times when we all need to exhibit compassion and feel someone's pain, but what we are talking about here goes way beyond that. The failure to own your emotions turns you into an emotional chameleon. Chameleons are those tiny lizards that take on the color of whatever they are perched on. When you actually take on the negative emotion that another person is experiencing, as though it were contagious, you are becoming an emotional chameleon. A Line Drawer is able to separate himself emotionally from another.

3. Your Thoughts Belong to You

No one can think your thoughts for you. No one can know your thoughts unless you choose to reveal them. You are 100 percent responsible for your thoughts. Mental boundaries are all about taking ownership of your thoughts and keeping them clean.

If you repeat belittling thoughts to yourself such as *I have no friends* or *I say the stupidest things,* then you will reap the expected consequences of those distorted thoughts: no one *will* like you! The saying "As he thinks in his heart, so is he" (Prov. 23:7 NKJV) is truer than most of us want to believe. You are the sum total of your thoughts. By the same token, you are responsible for keeping your mind clean and uncluttered. Be careful what you allow into your mind—music, movies, magazines, and so on. Distorted messages about love and romance create unrealistic expectations, and when real relationships don't live up to the ones portrayed by Hollywood or MTV videos, heartache and disappointment take over. It is crucial that you take charge of your thought life, reprogram your mind if it is full of self-condemning thoughts, and protect your eyes and ears from unrealistic and harmful subject matter.

Another aspect of owning your thoughts is not expecting others to read your mind. Molly never clued into this in her relationships. She always expected her friends to know her likes and dislikes and why she was in a bad mood. Her friends got tired of trying to play the role of an empathetic psychic. And Molly blamed everyone but herself for her loneliness, but she was the real problem.

This "if you really loved me you would know what I'm feeling" mentality is ludicrous. You can't expect or assume that a person can instinctively know what you are thinking or feeling at a given time. If you are upset or want to do a certain activity and no one is catching the clues, then just say it. Don't play charades if they don't get it. Learning how to take control of your thoughts and effectively express them to others will make your relationships run more smoothly.

4. Your Actions Belong to You

One of the most foolish things we attempt in relationships is to try to change the other person. You must be responsible for *your* behavior and let others be responsible for theirs.

A friend of mine once said, "You can't teach a pig how to sing. All you will do is frustrate yourself and irritate the pig." Apply that proverb to your dating relationships without hesitation. Is it really *your* job to try to change, mold, heal, fix, or reform the person you are with? Heck no! If you don't like what you see, then move on down the line, because it is sinful and wrong to oppress other people by trying to control them. Don't hack off the pig and bang your head against the wall.

Four Lies People Believe About Boundaries

The whole concept of relational boundaries is sometimes difficult to understand and apply. As a matter of fact, many of us believe certain things about boundaries that are simply not true. Here is a list of the top four lies people believe about boundaries.

Lie #1: Boundaries Are Walls

If you think setting boundaries is a way of putting up walls, you have totally misunderstood. That is not our point at all. *Walls* keep others out; walls isolate. Walls are bad. On the other hand, *drawing lines* lets others in, though with certain parameters for your safety. This is a way of making communication and friendships better because it helps others know how to relate to you and get to know you in the best manner.

Lie #2: Boundaries Are Selfish

Granted, we all struggle with selfishness. Selfishness means being "all about me." Selfishness entails excessive concern with yourself and your own needs without regard for others. Consider this statement from Scripture: "Do not let selfishness or pride be your guide. Instead, be humble and give more honor to others than to yourselves. Do not be interested only in your own life, but be interested in the lives of others" (Phil. 2:3–4).

But setting boundaries is *not* selfish. Setting boundaries merely forces you to take responsibility for yourself and your own needs, but at no point does this require you to ignore others' needs.

> **People who have a good sense of their own boundaries . . . are more in touch with the boundaries of others.**

Here's the shocker: people who have a good sense of their own boundaries and how to set them are *more in touch* with the boundaries of others. That's right! You are more equipped to serve others when your sense of self is grounded in a knowledge of who God is and who you are in Him and you have set appropriate boundaries based on this knowledge. Being secure, you are free to turn your attention to appropriate interaction with others. You serve them by respecting the lines they've drawn.

Lie #3: Boundaries Are Controlling and Manipulative

You don't like controlling, manipulative behavior? Neither do we. Line drawing liberates people from control and manipulation. Assert your boundaries in relationships, and let others take responsibility for their own lives.

You have the choice to allow or not to allow certain behaviors within a relationship. As an example, if you are on the phone with someone who constantly criticizes and abuses you, and that person refuses to change this behavior, you hang up. There is nothing controlling about that. Boundaries keep others from manipulating you.

Lie #4: Boundaries Are Insensitive and Rude

If you have come away with the belief that it is okay to do whatever you want whenever you want because it's your life, consider this: we most certainly do have an effect on others; therefore, we should always be sensitive to how our actions affect the lives of other people. But we cannot take responsibility for how others feel. You are responsible *to* others, but you are only responsible *for* yourself. There is a tremendous difference between these two.

> **You are responsible to others, but you are only responsible for yourself.**

The classic example is when a person avoids ending a relationship because he or she is afraid of hurting someone's feelings. If you know it is time to end a relationship, the most loving and sensitive thing you can do is break up. You are responsible to break up in a caring, compassionate manner, but you are not responsible for the other person's emotional reactions. And besides, the nature of a breakup is hurt feelings—it is normal to experience loss.

Consequences of Breaking This Commandment

- You will feel used and controlled by the people you're with.
- You will feel frustrated, confused, and angry because you let others determine how you feel.
- You will suffer emotional and physical harm because you did not draw the line when it came to protecting your body.

Benefits of Keeping
This Commandment

- You will build great friendships and still maintain a healthy sense of self.
- You will feel more secure for taking ownership of your body, emotions, and thoughts.
- You will be in control of your own schedule and how you spend your time.

Help for You Who Have Broken
This Commandment

- Stop taking responsibility for others' lives.
- Practice saying no with people you can trust.
- Let others speak for themselves, and stop speaking for others.
- Don't let your entire world revolve around the person you are dating.

Still Don't Believe Us?
Check This Out:

- "Go from the presence of a foolish man, When you do not perceive in him the lips of knowledge" (Prov. 14:7 NKJV).
- "So be very careful how you live. Do not live like those who are not wise, but live wisely" (Eph. 5:15).
- "Don't follow the ways of the wicked; don't do what evil people do. Avoid their ways, and don't follow them. Stay away from them and keep on going" (Prov. 4:14–15).

Thou Shalt Save Sex for Later

Britney Spears kisses Madonna. Howard Stern interviews naked dwarves. Girls Gone Wild commercials beset our TV screens. Society—particularly the media—has pushed the value of sex to an all-time low. No subject is more talked about, written about, studied, researched, and practiced than sex. The tragedy is that in spite of all this time and attention to sex, people still don't have a clue as to what it's really about.

> **Does God really have our best interests in mind when He tells us to wait?**

Society's party line on sex is simply, "If it feels right, do it. . . . Just be sure to use a condom." Meanwhile, the church is saying, "Whatever you do, don't have sex until you get married—that's the law." Whom should you listen to—society or the church?

Obviously, as Christians, we believe that you should save sex for marriage, case closed. But you may be wondering why God would tell us to do something so contrary to our natural urges and desires—does He really have our best interests in mind when He tells us to wait? In this chapter we'll look at God's perspective on sex and the reasons He tells us to stay pure in this arena.

As the old saying goes, "Sex is first between the ears before it's ever between the legs." For this reason, it's imperative that we look at our mind-set and our assumptions about sex. In other words, it's important that you understand society's take on sex and learn to think for yourself on the matter. After that, we'll give you some practical ways you can make it a lot easier on yourself to save sex for later. But first, let's pull back and take a look at the big picture.

God's Take on Sex

1. God Knows Sex

Most people think that God is clueless and naive about sex. However, nothing could be further from the truth. God knows sex. God knows more about sex than any *Seventeen* columnist or MTV relational guru. Think about it: if God created this entire world, and He created you and me, then God is the creator and designer of sex. Sex is God's idea! God is *the Sex Expert*. If Bill Gates gave you advice on how to make your computer run better, would you listen? Sure. So if God, the creator of sex, gives you information on what sex is all about, you'd be *crazy* not to listen. Therefore, lose the idea that God is sexually clueless. He is the *only one* who can clue you in on what sex is really all about.

> **God knows more about sex than any Seventeen columnist or MTV relational guru.**

2. God Says Sex Is Good

Imagine Adam and Eve rushing through the Garden of Eden to make love down by the crystal-clear river. When God looked over the balcony of heaven and saw them having sex right there on the riverbank, do you think He covered his eyes and said, "Ooh, yuck, what in the world are you doing?" No. I believe God had a smile on his face. He created sex to be a beautiful expression of love between a man and a woman in the fully committed relationship called marriage. Too many people think of God as antisex and prudish, but in truth God is prosex—within the proper context of marriage. Genesis 1:27 states that your maleness or femaleness (your sex organs) reflect the image of God. This does not mean that God has human parts, but that your sexuality is a reflection of the nature of God. When two people become one in the act of sexual intercourse, this is a picture of the oneness that God the Father, God the Son, and God the Holy Spirit share in the relationship of the Trinity.

3. God Designed Sex for a Reason

God is a purpose-driven Being. There is a reason for everything He has created and everything He does. He never does anything just for the heck of it. God designed sex for many reasons: First, sex is *unitive*—it creates union. God designed sex to be a physical act with deep social, spiritual, and psychological implications. Sex is a life-uniting act that must be coupled with the life-uniting commitment called marriage. Sex symbolizes that a man and a woman are now one physically, spiritually, economically, and socially. Second, sex is for procreation (making babies). God designed sex to be the means by which you and I came into this world. Third, sex is for pleasure. God didn't make the penis and the vagina numb like a callus on the bottom of your foot. God made our bodies responsive to touch because He loves us and wants us to enjoy the experience of sex.

4. God Realizes That Sex Is Bigger Than You Think (It's a Spiritual Thing!)

Most of us never really think that much about sex. *"Now wait a minute, Ben and Sam, you guys are way out of touch . . . I think about sex all the time!"* What we mean is, most people—parents, teachers, and coaches included—don't think about sex on a deep, cosmic, or spiritual level. Put on your thinking cap for a moment. If our sexual parts are a reflection of the nature and character of God, and if sexual intercourse itself is not only unitive, baby producing, and pleasurable, but is also a reflection of the triune God that we worship, then sex is a whole lot bigger than you think. Sex is much more about who God is than who we are. Therefore, we must respect it. It's like the sun: the world needs the sun in order to function, but if you look into the sun long enough you will burn your eyes, and if you stay out in it too long you'll get burned. We respect the sun because it's bigger and more powerful than we are. How much more, then, should we respect sex since it is a reflection of the very nature of God and points us to the reality of who He is. We must learn to appreciate the spiritual nature of sexuality and regain a sense of awe and reverence for this wonderful gift.

> **Sex is much more about who God is than who we are.**

5. God Tells You to Save Sex

God knows that sex is bigger and more powerful than you and I ever imagined. That's why He tells us to save it for marriage. God knows the catastrophic consequences of having sex outside of marriage. Not only can sex outside of marriage get you pregnant, fill you with guilt and shame, and give you a disease that will stay with you for life, but it will also cause you to miss the blessings that sex was created to bring to our lives.

If your brain is hurting from thinking about sex on this level, relax. Take a break, put an ice pack on your mind, and read on. We're going to bring it back to a level that anyone could understand.

Why Saving Sex Makes Sense

Saving sex for marriage makes logical sense. It's foolish to give your body, your soul, and your heart away to someone who really doesn't care about you. *But he says he loves me, that one day we will get married, that it will make us closer.* That's a bunch of bologna! If he really cares about you (and himself), he'll want to wait. Check out this list of even more reasons why saving sex for marriage is the best choice.

1. You Experience Wholeness

Across the street from where I work is a grocery store called "Whole Foods." They sell quality food products that are rich in nutrients and good for your body. Saving sex for later is like shopping at the "Whole Souls" store. Abstinence is health food for your body and your soul. When you say *no* to premarital sex, you are also saying *yes* to your spiritual and emotional wholeness. Sex outside of marriage is like binging on junk food for breakfast, lunch, and dinner. You'll eventually get fat and die of malnutrition. There's no doubt that sex within the context of marriage is wonderful and beautiful, but outside of that protective context, it's misleading and ugly. The more you continue to value your body and sexuality by waiting, the more peace and wholeness you will experience. Have you ever looked at someone and thought, *Man, that person has it all together*? If you desire to have it "all together," stay firm in your commitment to wait. We've talked to hundreds, maybe thousands, of men engaged to be married. Not one of them has ever said, "Yeah, what I want in a bride is a woman who's slept around a lot in high school and college. You know, a woman who knows her way around the bedroom." No, these men want a pure woman who respects herself and her future partner enough to wait. Men, ladies desire the same thing in you. No one wants to marry a player.

2. Your Self-Esteem Will Be Higher

Author and sex guru Rick Stedman says that this wholeness can only be achieved by practicing what he calls "temporary celibacy"(i.e., saving sex for marriage). "Sexual celibacy is the decision that sexuality is of value and personhood is special. When celibate, students are saying through their actions, 'I will not reduce my sexuality to a cheap giveaway. I will not pretend it is unimportant or insignificant. It is valuable and I am valuable. I will assert myself and my value by saving myself until marriage.'"[1] Stedman believes that saving sex for marriage increases your sense of self-worth and value. Saving sex has emotional and spiritual benefits as well—you gain a sense of purity and inner peace. When you feel good about the decisions you are making, you are not scattered or worried, and your self-esteem will naturally increase.

3. You Avoid Dangerous or Deadly Diseases

A while back I counseled a woman who had sex with a guy just one time—*one time*—and contracted HIV. She eventually died. I've prayed with people who were completely broken and emotionally devastated because they had had sex and contracted herpes, a sexually transmitted disease (STD) for which there is no cure. (By the way, herpes gives you nice, noticeable sores on your mouth aside from the ones on your sexual parts.) There are over twenty STDs.[2] Some of these diseases make it impossible for you to have children later on and can increase your risk for cervical cancer. Others can even kill you. According to a study of STDs among young Americans, "teenagers and young adults account for nearly half the cases of sexually transmitted diseases in the

United States, though they make up just a quarter of the sexually active population."[3] Even if you don't think you have an STD, you can't be sure: some of these diseases and their side effects don't make themselves known until later. So if a guy tells you he doesn't have HIV or herpes or any other of the twenty STDs, don't believe him. Why? Because more than likely he has not been tested and doesn't really know whether or not he is disease free. *If you think we are trying to scare you, then you're right.* We've seen people die from STDs, and we've seen others have to live with the nasty, devastating side effects. Who wants to die or have a gross disease for life?

> **Even if you don't think you have an STD, you can't be sure.**

4. You Value Your Body (Past, Present, and Future)

Another reason it makes logical sense to save sex for marriage is that you value your own body. If someone gave you a one-of-a-kind, $200,000 wedding dress that had been worn by a former princess from England, would you put it on to go out with your friends to the movies? No way. You'd save that dress for a very special day—like your wedding day. Nothing can cheapen an expensive, antique wedding dress like a root beer stain on the train or Junior Mint marks on the veil. The same principle applies to your body. If you value your body—hands, feet, penis, and vagina included—you will save it for your mate. Don't cheapen yourself. Continue to value your physical, emotional, and spiritual health by staying pure all the way to the altar. God says your body is a temple of the Holy Spirit and that you should honor Him with it. Most of you already know this and value the purity and body that God gave you, but it always helps to be reminded.

Saving sex makes sense because of Diet Coke. Let me explain: When I was a kid, the slogan for Coke was "It's the real thing." But as years passed and Americans put on the pounds, Diet Coke was invented. Diet Coke, like all diet drinks, is *not* the real thing. Why? Because of the aftertaste. Diet Coke may look like the real thing, feel like the real thing, and taste like the real thing for a while, but soon the aftertaste shouts to your mouth, "This ain't the real thing!" It's the same with premarital sex. The aftertaste of sex: getting pregnant, having an abortion, contracting HIV, scattering yourself emotionally—not to mention the bitter experience of shame, guilt, and regret—underscores the reality that *this ain't the real thing*. If you are one of the millions of students who have decided to wait, forge on in the journey and continue to experience the wholeness, peace, and self-worth that God is sending your way.

Okay, you know it's smart and right to save yourself for marriage. You've experienced a sense of value and a higher self-esteem for doing so. But what in the world do you do with all of your sexual desires in the meantime? It's not as if God turns off your sexual desires like a light switch when you decide to save sex for marriage, then flips the switch to "on" when you say "I do" ten or fifteen years down the road. We will go into greater detail on this issue in Commandment Seven. In the meantime, here are six crucial guidelines to help you hold fast to your resolve.

How to Save Sex for Later

1. Make a Real Commitment

Sun Tzu, in his classic book *The Art of War,* said that "every battle is won before it's ever fought." In other words, winning any battle is all about *preparation*. It's the decisions you make *before* you get into the heat of battle that give you the victory. The same applies to sex and sexual purity. The commitment you make *today* not to give away your body until you are married will enable you to stay pure until that special day. It's never too late to say *no* and walk away even in the heat of battle. But saying *yes* to waiting *now*, before you even go on that first date, will make it easier for you to stay strong. Even better, get together with your closest friends, and make a pact to keep one other accountable. Make a commitment to stay pure, value your body, and save sex for the context of marriage. Be a real woman, or a real man. Make this commitment and stick to it no matter what.

> It's the decisions you make **before** you get into the heat of battle that give you the victory.

2. Only Go Out with Like-minded Believers

The commitment to stay pure goes hand in hand with a commitment to date fellow believers in Christ. We say, "like-minded," because they must share your specific views of sexual purity and your desire to save sex for marriage. Don't even entertain the thought of going out with an unbeliever. *Well, it's just one date . . . it's no big deal.* Wrong. It *is* a big deal. I know of a young lady who traces the downward spiral of her life to when she began to go out with non-Christian guys. Eventually she found herself in the wrong place with the wrong guy and lost her virginity by date rape. Don't compromise your standards and go out with someone who doesn't follow God's commandments on sex.

3. Don't Drink or Go Out with Someone Who Does Drink

Too many people, both young and old, do stupid, embarrassing, and many times fatal things while under the influence of alcohol. It's nearly impossible to go through high school without losing a friend to an alcohol-related shooting or car wreck. And another practical tip for staying pure: don't drink or hang out with the crowd who does. If you know there is going to be drinking at someone's home or party, don't go there. Don't go out or get in a car with someone who's drinking. Why people think they need an artificial substance to have fun is beyond me. Trust me, you can have a blast without the booze. Would you want to wake up in your own vomit or have a hellacious hangover, much less do something sexually that you wouldn't do if you were sober?

4. Listen to Your Parents—Not Your So-Called "Friends"

Your parents care a lot more about you than your peers. If your parents tell you not to go out with someone, listen to them. Believe it or not, they see things that you cannot. One day you will be saying the same things to your kids. If your parents talk to you about purity and how important and beneficial it is, take note. They have been where you are today and have faced, for the most part, the same issues, longings, desires, and decisions you're facing. Plus, the only commandment in the real Ten Commandments that also makes a promise is the one that tells you to honor your mom and dad.

5. Trust God's Take on Sex

The issue of sexual purity boils down to this: Who are you going to trust, God or this godless society? God loves you even more than your parents or your best friend. When He says to save sex for marriage, He's not trying to rain on your parade. God knows where you can experience maximum sexual fulfillment and pleasure—that's marriage. God also knows that when you have sex before you get married, you run the risk of getting pregnant, contracting a disease, and having your heart and body used up and discarded, like a piece of trash. God desires that you experience wholeness, peace, self-respect, and lasting feelings of self-worth. Trust that God knows what's best for you. Make that commitment to purity, and you will reap lasting benefits for years to come.

6. Receive Forgiveness

It's difficult to celebrate wholeness if you feel unforgiven. You may need healing in the sexual arena. One of the most powerful ways to experience real forgiveness is to observe how Jesus Christ treated persons who were caught in the web of sexual promiscuity. We'll talk more in the next chapter about forgiveness and how Christ handled sexual sin.

Consequences of Breaking This Commandment

- You will sacrifice the sense of wholeness and purity that God desires for you to have.
- You will tarnish the experience of sex as it's intended.

Benefits of Keeping This Commandment

- You will experience maximum wholeness and a healthy sense of self-respect.
- You will enjoy sex inside of marriage—the way God intended it to be.

Help for You Who Have Broken This Commandment

- Make a commitment to become a "born-again virgin" and to save sex until you are married.
- Confess your past mistakes and receive the grace and forgiveness of God.
- Set clear boundaries for physical intimacy before you get involved in another relationship.

Still Don't Believe Us?
Check This Out:

- "So run away from sexual sin. Every other sin people do is outside their bodies, but those who sin sexually sin against their own bodies. You should know that your body is a temple for the Holy Spirit who is in you. You have received the Holy Spirit from God. So you do not belong to yourselves, because you were bought by God for a price. So honor God with your bodies" (1 Cor. 6:18–20).

- "Marriage is to be held in honor among all, and the marriage bed is to be undefiled; for fornicators and adulterers God will judge" (Heb. 13:4 NASB).

- "Watch over your heart with all diligence, for from it flow the springs of life" (Prov. 4:23 NASB).

Commandment 7

Thou Shalt Not Fall for Sex Lies

E rika Harold knows what she wants out of life. She is a Phi Beta Kappa graduate of the University of Illinois and was a member of *USA Today*'s 2000 All-USA College Academic Team. This three-time member of the National Dean's List has been accepted to Harvard Law School, where she will begin her studies during the fall of 2004. Here's what she has to say about sex before marriage:

> Ever since I can remember, I've had a commitment to abstinence. I was fortunate enough to be raised by two loving parents who encouraged me to set high standards, to value myself, and to save sex for marriage. But I grew up knowing that I was lucky and that not every young person had the love and support that I did. I saw many of my peers use sex to try to find that love and acceptance. But instead of being able to fill that void, many of them became teen parents, contracted diseases, and had their hearts broken.[1]

Tragically, not everyone holds Erika's views on purity. I will never forget a phone call I received from an angry young girl named Michelle. She had heard me give a talk on why sex before marriage is not only wrong but is also a stupid choice to make.

"You can't discourage people who want to have sex. You need to teach people to have safe sex and have it with someone they love. I think that's really all that matters," she declared in a defensive tone. After calming her down and explaining the reasons for my stance, I saw her resolve begin to break, and she eventually opened up to reveal the real issue she was hiding.

"I can't stop messing around with my boyfriend. We've tried to stop 'cause it's against our beliefs, but we just can't stop doing it. It's like a drug. Whenever we are together we just want to fool around," she said in between sobs. Then she hung up the phone.

There are many teenagers like Michelle. They crave intimacy but don't know how to express this desire in a healthy way. Some students swim in dangerous sexual waters because they have fallen for one of the many "sex lies" flowing out of pop culture. Contrary to the mainstream message, "safe" sex (if there *is* such a thing) does *not* make you feel good about yourself or closer to the person you love. It actually destroys your self-esteem and plagues you with guilt and disappointment (not to mention the possible side effects: pregnancy, HIV, and herpes). In this chapter, you'll learn about the Seven Stupid Sex Lies, how to respond to these lies, and steps you can take to stay pure.

Seven Stupid Sex Lies

1. Everything but . . . Is Okay
(aka "The Lewinsky Loophole")

Like former president Bill Clinton, some have bought the lie that you can do anything you want with the opposite sex as long as it's not sexual intercourse (penis inserted into vagina), and you are still pure and okay. Imagine two couples at a party. After a while of mixing and mingling, Couple A decides to sneak away to an upstairs bedroom as the party rocks on. They start with a kiss, and before long they are losing clothes left and right. They are physically intimate in every way except actual intercourse. About the same time, Couple B makes their escape from the crowd downstairs and finds a bedroom down the hall. They start with a kiss, and before long they too are losing clothes left and right. The passion progresses to full sexual intercourse.

Now when God looks down from heaven at this party, what is His response? Do you think He'd be disappointed in Couple B for going "all the way," then turn around and say, "But that Couple A . . . they sure are holy. Whew, they stopped just in time! No harm there"?

2. If You're in Love, It's Okay

Tears pour down the face of a seventeen-year-old girl who has fallen for the oldest line in the book, lost her virginity, and been dropped in less time than Britney's Vegas marriage lasted. She said, "We were going to get married. We were going to go to the same college. I thought he really loved me." Some people believe that if you've dated someone for a while, if you're in love, and if marriage is a possibility in the future, then sex is okay. Guys dangle the "this-is-forever" carrot in front of girls as a means of luring them into bed. How many girls have shed tears after it was too late—when they've already given in to their urges and his lies? If someone really loves you, he will respect you enough to wait.

3. It Will Make Us Closer

Sex is a bonding experience. It connects you with a person physically, emotionally, psychologically, and spiritually. However, whenever you have physical unification (sexual intercourse) without economic and social unification (aka marriage), you will always have guilt, shame, and the confusion that follows mixed signals in a relationship.

Look at what happened to sixteen-year-old Tonya. "My junior year in high school I started going out with one of the most popular guys in school. We really clicked, and I was so in love with him. He said he loved me and wanted to share everything with me by making love to me. I told him I wasn't ready for that and didn't think it was a good idea. He told me we would always be together and we should take our relationship to the next level by having sex. I finally gave in. The next day he began avoiding me and wouldn't return my calls. By the end of the week, he broke up with me. Then, if that wasn't bad enough, I found out he had slept with other girls in school, and I had gotten herpes from having sex with him just one time. I see him in the halls but he never speaks to me. Now he has a new girlfriend. That will probably last a few months, and now I have this new disease that will never go away."

> In the wrong context, sex . . . leaves you feeling empty, fragmented, and confused.

The Bible says you can't separate the physical from the emotional. In other words, you can't have sex with someone in the bedroom and leave your soul parked outside in the car. If you try this, your relationship will ultimately be torn apart, and your soul will be left with a gaping wound. In the wrong context, sex does not draw two people closer together, but leaves them feeling empty, fragmented, and confused.

4. You Won't Get Pregnant

Listen, you can get pregnant anytime you have sex with another person. You can get pregnant the first time you have sex. You can get pregnant using a condom. You can get pregnant during the menstrual cycle. You can get pregnant if you pull out before orgasm. You can get pregnant on the pill. You can get pregnant without even having sexual intercourse (check out *Sports Illustrated*'s article on the birth of NBA superstar Allen Iverson[2]). Outside of abstinence, there are no guarantees.

5. Everybody's Doing It

Recent surveys show that this is sheer nonsense. There are millions of young people who are waiting. The Centers for Disease Control has reported that 54.4 percent of teens are abstaining from sex.[3] When you consider the number of teens in the U.S., this translates to 10.7 million teens who are saving sex for marriage.[4] Another recent study indicates that the virginity rate among teens has been steadily rising over the last decade.[5] The truth is, *not* everybody's doing it. Granted, we are all susceptible to peer pressure, and it can definitely be difficult to step out of the mainstream and stand on our own. It can also be very tempting to check out the much-talked-about sex scene when our friends—and the culture in general—view us as clue-less, hopelessly dull, or just inept for abstaining.

Everybody does seem to be doing it! From Abercrombie & Fitch catalogs, to TV sitcoms, to your best friend, it's easy to get the impression that everyone is having sex. Because we are saturated by media buzz and gossip about who's-doing-what-with-whom, the legiti-macy and even promotion of extramarital sex is every-where we look.

> The truth is, not everybody's doing it.

While pop culture glam-orizes sex, it neglects to de-pict the carnage from casual couplings. It may be hard to swim upstream, and it might seem cool to swim mainstream, but the results are costly. The notion that "everybody's doing it" has only resulted in the escalation of STDs, broken hearts, ruptured marriages, and unwanted babies, not to mention a whole lot of grief.

6. All You Need Is a Condom

This lie states that if you want to have safe sex, meaning you don't want to die of a disease or produce a baby, then all you need is a condom. Here is the real truth about condoms.

Condoms fail at least 10 percent of the time to prevent pregnancy. Multiple studies involving monogamous couples using a condom during every single incident of intercourse for six to twelve months have shown that *the condom failure rate is at least 10 percent, if not more.* That's for couples participating in a scientific study who had to use condoms every single time they had sex. In the real world, people tend to be more careless.[6]

In the study, one out of ten women became pregnant even though her partner used a condom every time they had sex. What is so startling about this statistic? The fact that a woman can only get pregnant a few days of the month! During the woman's window of fertility each month, which is only about five days, the condoms are failing 10 percent of the time.

Condoms fail more than 10 percent of the time to prevent STDs. Do you know anyone who really would willingly place one bullet in a chamber of a revolver, spin the chamber, place the barrel in his mouth, and then pull the trigger? The very idea of being so reckless with a life is strange and frightening.

Catch this: while the odds of getting HIV or some other STD are not as great as one out of six (as with Russian roulette), *they are not far behind.* Based on condom failure rate for pregnancy, your sexual roulette odds with the condom are one out of ten. The problem is that HIV, unlike pregnancy, can strike each and every day of the month. If condoms failed 10 percent of the time for pregnancy, how often must and do they fail for HIV when infection is possible any day, any time?

Is this just a scare tactic to try to convince you not to have sex? No. Research the facts yourself. The numbers may vary from study to study, but today no medical authorities dispute

> **Condoms do not fit over your mind, heart, and soul.**

the fact that truly safe sex is *impossible* apart from abstinence.

Condoms do not fit over your mind, heart, and soul. To tell people that using a condom will protect them from the dangers of sex is like telling someone to put on a glove made of asbestos and then stand for a few moments in a fiery furnace. The hand may not be singed, but the hair and flesh of the rest of the body will be cooked. Likewise, you may not get burned by pregnancy, STDs, or AIDS, but condoms won't prevent the mental, emotional, and spiritual burns left by sex.

Your sexuality involves the totality of who you are and the totality of your partner. You can choose to block off your mind or heart or soul during a sexual act, but the bonding aspects (and consequent ripping effects when the relationship terminates) may slip in "under the radar." You may not be consciously aware that bonding is occurring, but the condom, which offers a degree of protection from pregnancy and STDs, does not offer a smidgen of protection for your soul.

7. Abortion Is Just a Medical Procedure

Some people hold a casual and naive attitude about abortion, saying, "No big deal . . . if I get pregnant I'll just have an abortion." Abortion is murder; it's not "just a medical procedure." Not only are you taking an innocent life, you are also endangering yourself in many ways. Abortion is inherently unsafe. Check out what David C. Reardon, author of *Making Abortion Rare*, says:

> Well over a hundred significant physical and psychological complications have been linked to abortion. This list of complications is quite diverse. One cross-sectional sample would include

increased rates of breast cancer, sterility, substance abuse, and sexual dysfunctions. An equally interesting cross-section, which parallels the first, would include increased rates of liver cancer, ectopic pregnancies, suicide attempts, and broken relationships. The psychological effects of abortion can be particularly devastating, literally crippling a woman's ability to function in normal relationships with family or friends, and even at work. The frequency and severity of abortion-related complications have led some critics of abortion, including myself, to conclude that the phrase "safe abortion" is an oxymoron.[7]

An edition of *Southern Medical Journal* cites that 42.6 percent of teenage moms who undergo abortions suffer some kind of damage to their reproductive organs and that 74 percent suffer incomplete operations and subsequent passage of the baby's body parts and tissue.[8]

Don't buy the deadly lie that abortion is a harmless quick fix!

How Do You Respond to the Lies?

What do you do if you find yourself in a situation where someone tries to manipulate you with one of these lies? In other words, when someone comes on to you in an inappropriate manner, how do you respond and tell him or her to take a hike?

Here are some ideas on how to say "no":

- Don't let the other person think that you are depriving them of something. It is their problem if they want to put themselves at risk for diseases and pregnancy.

- End the discussion quickly. After you've firmly said *no,* move on to talking about something else.

Here are some comebacks to common come-on lines:

The Come-On	The Comeback
Trust me. I won't let anything happen to you.	You don't have control over the whole situation. You don't know what is going to happen afterward, and I don't want to take the risk.
I've been tested, and I'm clean.	It's nice that you've been tested, but I'm looking for someone who doesn't need to be tested because they are waiting, like me. Besides, STDs aren't the only consequence of having sex. There is also the possibility of pregnancy, and I'm definitely not ready to be a teenage mom!
But I love you. Don't you love me?	Love has nothing to do with it. I *respect* myself enough to wait.
Show me how much you love me.	I am showing you how much I love you by waiting.
No one will find out about this.	I will, and people knowing will be the least of my problems if I get a disease or have a baby.
It will bring us closer together.	If anything, it will make things more complicated and tear us apart.
If you won't have sex with me, I'll just find someone who will.	Go ahead. Find someone who doesn't respect you or him- or herself.

The Come-On	The Comeback
I'll break up with you if you don't have sex with me.	How sad that you are only with me to have sex. Now that I know this, it looks like you're doing me a favor dumping me.
It's okay; I've got a condom.	Condoms aren't 100 percent effective against STDs and pregnancy, and they provide zero protection from the emotional hurt I could suffer.
I'll always love you. Let me share this with you.	If you will always love me, then it won't make a difference if we wait until I'm ready.

© 2002 Worth the Wait®

Say *yes* to purity now. Make a real commitment, and be ready to respond in situations that could cause you to compromise your standards. If you find yourself tempted to go too far, even if you are in the heat of the moment, just get up and leave. Run. Get out of there! That's what Joseph did in the Bible when Pharoah's wife kept coming on to him. He got the heck out of the house and sprinted down the road.

Actions You Can Take to Stay Pure

1. Celebrate the Power of Purity

First, make the decision to commit to purity, and then fully embrace this powerful choice. There is a power in purity. You are making the best choice in saving sex for later. You are feeding your mind and body healthy soul food. Remember the Diet Coke effect

(Chapter 6). Don't be a wimp about it. Celebrate it. Celebrate the value you have to God, to yourself, and to others. Celebrate the power you feel by saying *no* to instant and fleeting gratification and *yes* to the kind that lasts.

2. Don't Go Out with Someone Who's a Lot Older Than You

You are asking for trouble when you go out with someone who's more than two years older than you. Some make this big-time mistake when an older guy or older girl comes on to them. Too often, all the older person wants is to lead the younger one down the path of sexual temptation. Girls, you must be especially aware of this.

3. Don't Pray Together

Prayer binds you more closely to another person than anything else can. Don't let some guy knowingly or unknowingly use "spirituality" to manipulate you by using the old "let's pray together" line. With the exception of praying at meals or in a group setting, don't go there.

4. Watch How You Dress

Let's face it, guys are turned on by what they see. If you run around dressed like you are auditioning for a Shakira or Christina Aguilera video, you send the wrong message. A lot of girls don't understand the way God has wired guys, and they unwittingly seduce them by the revealing way they dress. Girls, be smart and dress like a lady, not like a tramp.

5. Stay Away from Porn

Looking at pornography is a quick way to simultaneously lose your soul as well as your respect for the opposite sex. Porn distorts the value and image of what real love and sex are all about. Looking at pornography is like trying to quench your thirst by drinking salt water from the ocean. It may provide an illusion of fulfillment, but it only leaves you empty and wanting more. Also, when you engage in porn, the laws of addiction take hold—the more you look at it, the more enslaved and less satisfied you become. Just as pot smokers get tired of pot and want to move on to stronger drugs, such as crack, porn watchers move from soft-core stuff to hard-core stuff.

> **Pornography may provide an illusion of fulfillment, but it only leaves you empty and wanting more.**

If you struggle with this temptation, ask a parent or trusted youth pastor, teacher, or coach for help.

6. Don't Be Home Alone

You should never *ever* go over to someone's house or apartment if his or her parents are not there. Don't make exceptions here, such as "Well, my folks will be back in a little while," or "We won't do anything except watch TV." Rationalizations like these only get you into trouble. Always be sure a mom or dad is home when you're with someone.

7. Do Things in Groups

There is safety in numbers. If you spend too much one-on-one time with your boyfriend or girlfriend, you'll eventually run out of things to talk about. Don't drop all your friends and overdose on the dating

> **There is safety in numbers.**

thing. Stay balanced, keep your friends, and go out in groups as much as you can.

So Just How Far Is Too Far?

For some of you, this is the wrong question to ask. Your motivations are impure and your focus is on how much you can get away with. If this describes you, take another look at Commandment One: "Thou Shalt Get a Life." For others, this is a very legitimate question at this point in your life. You know that God has created you with normal desires for affection and touch, and yet you resolve to maintain your purity. Here are the guidelines:

1. Sexual Intercourse Outside of Marriage Is Too Far

Just in case you missed it, sex is reserved for marriage, even if you think you will marry, or if you really love each other. Sex with someone who is not currently your husband or wife is wrong.

2. Oral Sex Is Too Far

The Bible says not to have a hint of sexual impurity, and oral sex is much more than a hint. Oral sex outside of marriage is degrading and is way out of bounds. Some try to "cheat" the system by limiting their sexual encounters. They substitute with oral sex and yet end up having just as much guilt and hurt in their souls. Remember, sex is not just a series of physical acts. It involves the soul.

3. Touching Someone Below the Neck Is Too Far

Anytime you let someone touch you on your breasts or on your genital area (penis, vagina, etc.), you are going too far. This is called "foreplay," which means you are preparing your body and your partner's body for intercourse. So don't kid yourself with the "everything but intercourse is okay" attitude.

If we haven't spelled it out clearly enough, this should suffice: anything outside of kissing or nonsexual touch is going too far. For some people, kissing may even be going too far. Why? Because the issue is a *heart* issue. Jesus addressed this in Matthew 5:28 when He said, "But I tell you that if anyone looks at a woman and wants to sin sexually with her, in his mind he has already done that sin with the woman." When in doubt, ask yourself three questions:

1. What are the motivations of my heart?

2. Does this respect the other person?

3. Will this lead me to "out-of-control" behavior?

I've Already Gone Too Far—Now What?

Listen, it's never too late to do the right thing. If you have gone too far physically, tell your parents. In addition, you may need to tell a trusted youth worker (of the same gender) what has happened. If you think you are pregnant or have a disease, be sure to talk to your mom or dad, or go see your family doctor immediately.

Just because you have gone too far doesn't mean you have to go there again. Confess your sin to God and ask Him to forgive you. You must understand that forgiveness does not equal permission. In other words, don't say, "Hey, I can mess around now and everything will be okay because God will forgive me." Going too far sexually *always* has consequences. Don't buy into the lie that says you can fool around now and be forgiven later. Speaking of forgiveness, let's talk more about that.

Receive Forgiveness

Look at how Christ dealt with folks who went too far sexually. When Jesus met the woman at the well who had been divorced four times and was currently shacking up with someone, He didn't condemn her. He didn't condone her actions either. Instead, He told her where she could find living water.

When some religious fundamentalists caught a woman in the very act of adultery and threw her naked into the dirty streets to be stoned to death, Jesus didn't join them. Instead, He stooped down and drew in the sand. Then He stood up and said, "Anyone here who has never sinned can throw the first stone at her" (John 8:7). Everyone backed off, leaving Jesus with the frightened woman. He then turned back to the woman and asked her, "Woman, where are they? Has no one judged you guilty? . . . I also don't judge you guilty. You may go now, but don't sin anymore" (John 8:10–11).

When a prostitute poured out perfume on Jesus' feet in the middle of a Bible study, what did He do? He forgave her and said to the judgmental people looking on, "I tell you that her many sins are forgiven, so she showed great love. But the person who is forgiven only a little will love only a little" (Luke 7:47).

You can experience this kind of forgiveness. First, acknowledge that you've messed up. Just tell God how you feel about your sexual past. Confess how you've devalued yourself by scattering yourself sexually. Receive His forgiveness. If the God who made you and placed value on you says, "You are forgiven, you are whole," then what do you have to fear or dread?

The longer you practice purity and renewing your mind with God's forgiveness, the more forgiven you will feel. It often takes time for our hearts and emotions to catch up with what our minds know to be true.

A Final Word

You don't have to sell yourself short sexually. If you've made a pledge for abstinence, you're in good company. Remember the brainy Erika Harold at the beginning of this chapter? Did we forget to mention that she's also drop-dead gorgeous and was crowned Miss America for 2003? When she was asked how she wanted to be remembered after her reign as Miss America 2003, she said she wanted people to say, "She was the one who stood up for what she believed in."[9]

How do you want to be remembered?

Consequences of Breaking This Commandment

- You are at risk of contracting an STD or becoming pregnant.
- You will experience momentary gratification followed by intense feelings of guilt, shame, and regret.
- You will lose your self-respect, as well as true security in your relationships.
- You won't be able to trust someone who is willing to sacrifice your integrity for his or her momentary pleasure.

Benefits of Keeping This Commandment

- You will have healthier and more fulfilling dating relationships built on foundations that last.
- You will be able to distinguish between someone who really cares and has your best interest in mind and someone who selfishly puts his desires over what's best for the relationship.
- You will enjoy sex inside of marriage the way God intended it to be.

Help for You Who Have Broken This Commandment

- Make a commitment to become a "born-again virgin" and to save sex until you are married.
- Confess your past mistakes and receive the grace and forgiveness of God.
- Set clear boundaries for physical intimacy before you get involved in another relationship.

Still Don't Believe Us? Check This Out:

- "Those who belong to Christ Jesus have crucified their own sinful selves. They have given up their old selfish feelings and the evil things they wanted to do" (Gal. 5:24).
- "Therefore do not let sin reign in your mortal body that you should obey its lusts, and do not go on presenting the members of your body to sin as instruments of unrighteousness; but present yourselves to God as those alive from the dead, and your members as instruments of righteousness to God" (Rom. 6:12–13 NASB).
- "So put all evil things out of your life: sexual sinning, doing evil, letting evil thoughts control you, wanting things that are evil, and greed. This is really serving a false god . . . Everything you do or say should be done to obey Jesus your Lord. And in all you do, give thanks to God the Father through Jesus" (Col. 3:5, 17).

Commandment 8

Thou Shalt Not Ignore Warning Signs

On the night of April 14, 1912, one of the greatest disasters of all time occurred when the HMS *Titanic*, on her maiden voyage, struck an iceberg and sank in a matter of hours. More than fifteen hundred men, women, and children were swallowed by the ocean, never to be seen again. The captain and crew knew in advance that it was too dangerous to be sailing in that region that night. This tragedy could have been avoided. The *Titanic* began receiving radio messages from other ships to look out for icebergs as early as Friday, April 12. By Sunday, the weather had grown colder, and the warnings were more frequent. Another steamer, only twenty miles away, called to warn that she was stopped and surrounded by ice. Also troubling was the fact that the men in the *Titanic*'s crow's nest, ordered to look out for ice, were never issued binoculars. In spite of all the warnings and the lack of preparation, the *Titanic* continued to cruise full speed ahead that fateful night. Caught up in the excitement of sailing this large, "unsinkable," luxurious ship, the captain failed to heed obvious warning signs along the way.

How many guys and girls have ended up drowning in the waters of heartache because they've ignored important warning signs and red flags about a relationship? How many young people experience heartbreak and regret because they fail to heed advice from parents and friends? Numerous indicators can warn of a dating relationship's impending doom. In this chapter we focus on *five major warning signs.*

More than likely, these warning signs are actually one-hundred-foot banners screaming, "GET OUT WHILE YOU CAN!" When you, your parents, or your friends see warning signs, red flags, or something else that makes you or them say, "Uh-oh," we suggest that you listen up and act *immediately.* Here is a list of the five warning signs you can't afford to ignore.

The Five Deadly Signs

Warning! The following comments concerning the five deadly signs are very harsh. We are committed to speaking the truth, and we make no apologies for our lack of "political correctness." We've seen too many victims of relational Titanics to be blasé. If it requires saying some hard truths in a sharp manner, so be it. Please understand that we have deep compassion for all the young people who struggle with any one or more of the five deadly signs. Hopefully these words can save you or someone you know from a lot of pain.

One more thing: *Our hope is that if you have any of these five problems, you will find help immediately by sharing with someone you trust, and then by seeking professional help.*

1. Abuse

One of the most destructive warning signs for a relationship is any form of abuse. Sadly, many people don't understand what abuse actually is. For example, most people think of abuse as only physical contact. However, abuse encompasses a broad range of aggressive behaviors, including physical, verbal, emotional, and sexual behavior. *All* of these forms of abuse can be equally damaging. Are you wondering how to define abuse? Take a look at these definitions adapted from materials published by the Austin Stress Clinic:

- *Physical abuse*—any use of size, strength, or presence to hurt or control someone.

- *Verbal abuse*—any use of words or voice to control or hurt another person.

- *Emotional abuse*—any action or lack of action meant to control or put down another.

- *Sexual abuse*—any sexual behavior, verbal or physical, engaged in without consent, which may be emotionally or physically harmful.

So while you may know that hitting, kicking, and choking are abuse, did you know that threats to hit or harm are also abusive? Are you aware that insults and name-calling qualify as abuse? Have you considered that intense jealousy and manipulation with lies are also abusive? How about criticism, intimidation, and humiliation?

There is no reasonable defense or explanation that can support any form of abuse—ever.

Abuse can take many forms, and sometimes it can even be quite subtle. Regardless of the form that it takes, abuse is never justified. There is no rationalization or excuse that could justify abusing another person. *There is no reasonable defense or explanation that can support any form of abuse—ever.* We are always astonished at the efforts to justify abuse. "But he didn't mean it," or "He's under a lot of stress," or "Maybe I pushed her to that point, and she just snapped." And the scariest response of all: "It's all right because I know it will never happen again." Don't bet on it!

So what do you do if you're dating someone who's abusive? Run. Now. Get away from that person now and ask questions later. You may be thinking, *Well, that sounds pretty harsh and unforgiving*. Yes, it is harsh, but that is your best response. We feel very strongly about the need to deal with this immediately.

Abuse of any kind involves two people, right? One to be abusive and one to be abused. Take away either person, and the abuse isn't happening anymore. If you find yourself frequently drawn to abusive people, refer back to the First Commandment: Thou Shalt Get a Life. Sometimes people (more often girls) are attracted to a guy or girl, not despite their abusive tendencies, but because of them. These girls may have low self-esteem and feel an unconscious need to be punished somehow. To be sure, there are a lot of different issues involved in low self-esteem. But one way to increase self-esteem and make yourself less vulnerable to abuse is to make your own life productive and fulfilling before you ever choose to date someone.

2. Addictions

By its very nature, an addiction is a powerful habit that cannot be overcome merely by a decision to stop. I guess it could be argued that we all have an addiction to something, whether it be caffeine, computers, TV, or more dangerous substances like alcohol, marijuana, or cocaine. For our purposes, let's focus on the latter group of addictions: alcohol and drugs.

Essentially, when you choose to date an addict, you are dealing with someone who is enslaved to a substance. It's impossible to have a healthy relationship with such a person. Period. That substance is his number one priority, and unless he gets help, it will always be his top priority. As long as that person is addicted, he is not going to have control of his life or have healthy relationships of any kind. That person has nothing to give because his energy and focus go to the drug or drink of choice. Do you really want to be with someone who is checked-out on life, obsessed, unpredictable, irresponsible, self-deceived, and deceptive? Of course not!

If the guy or girl you are interested in has one or a combination of these three signs, he or she is an addict: (1) he/she demonstrates a pattern of using a substance that alters chemistry or mood, (2) he/she spends a significant amount of time (daily or even every weekend) acquiring and consuming the drug of choice, and (3) he/she continues to use it despite the fact that the person's life is out of control and unmanageable, or that he or she is experiencing obvious physical or psychological effects (i.e., depression, anxiousness, problems at school).

> Do you really want to be with someone who is checked-out on life, obsessed, unpredictable, irresponsible, self-deceived, and deceptive?

The worst thing you can do for yourself and the addict is to do nothing and hope it goes away. You become part of the problem, and potentially a "coaddict" as the enabler of this behavior. First, get out of the dating relationship. You can't date someone who has an addiction—you'll be in way over your head. Be that person's friend, and with the help of other friends, a teacher, youth leader, or another trusted person, confront his or her behavior head-on. Try the tough love approach. Insist that your friend get help immediately through some form of recovery, individual counseling, or twelve-step group. If he or she is unwilling to get help, walk away. Remember, it is not your job to save that person.

3. Disrespectfulness

Okay, we don't care if we do sound like your grandmother. Another warning sign to look out for is disrespect toward others. Does your sweetheart have a real problem with people who are in charge? Does he, as your mom would say, "talk back" to his parents, coaches, or teachers? Does she think it's cool to constantly put other people down? Does he like to destroy stuff that's not his to be destroying? If you answered yes to any one of these questions, you may be dating a person with a real problem.

If the person you're dating can't respect others, there is a strong possibility that he or she has no respect for him- or herself, and it's just a matter of time before this person will have no respect for you. People with a pattern of disrespectfulness are usually arrogant, callous, demanding, and irresponsible. Their self-esteem is virtually nonexistent, so they see no need to esteem others. If you are already involved with someone like this, take heed: you may be flirting with one of the five deadly signs.

4. Emotional Baggage

The fourth deadly sign is what we call "emotional baggage." It is the guy or girl who carries significant, unresolved emotional or psychological baggage that interferes with normal, healthy relational functioning. From the outset we want to establish the fact that we all have some emotional baggage. So we are not saying you should only find someone who is free of all emotional issues (it's not going to happen in this lifetime). We *are* saying that you must beware of those who have little or no insight into their issues and subsequently have never resolved them.

Eileen was a beautiful, intelligent sixteen-year-old girl, captain of her cheerleading squad, and every boy's dream date. She had tons of friends, a bright future, and one very tragic secret. She was bulimic. So many things in her life were beyond her control—her parents' divorce, the pressure to make good grades, the expectation to be and look perfect—but she felt like her weight was one thing she could definitely control. And no one had to know. It would be her little secret.

Then along came Michael. He and Eileen started dating, and it didn't take Michael long to realize that Eileen was acting a little odd. When he tried, with some of Eileen's friends, to confront her, she blew up at them and told them they just didn't understand. She broke up with Michael, distanced herself from her friends, and became more and more enslaved to her sickness.

Eileen is someone who represents the fourth deadly sign—not because she has bulimia but because she has never taken the time to acknowledge the problem, understand the effects, and work toward some form of emotional healing. No doubt there are many who have struggled with an eating disorder or know someone who does. We have tremendous empathy for them. The truth we want to drive home is that you can't expect to have a healthy relationship with someone who carries a lot of "emotional baggage."

> You can't expect to have a healthy relationship with someone who carries a lot of "emotional baggage."

"So we all have issues . . . where do we go from here?" you ask. Remember that your friends' emotional issues only become "baggage" if they are not aware of their issues in the first place or if they have not begun the process of healing. When you've got a problem, your best response is to face it, acknowledge it, feel it, talk about it, and then do something about it. Don't be afraid to seek professional help, pastoral help, or some other form of support in order to address your issues.

5. Denial

The fifth and final warning sign comes when you, after reading this chapter and the previous chapters, have an understanding that there are serious concerns about the person you're going out with, but you can't seem to get out. You know it's wrong, but you simply will not heed the warning sign. Or you may find that you have a strong desire to break up, and yet something holds you back. There are others who might consider themselves the exception to the rule, minimizing, rationalizing, or just flat denying the truth. In any case, if you can identify with any of the above warning signs and you're still in the relationship, you are living out the fifth deadly sign. It's as though you're driving down a road in broad daylight. You suddenly notice orange cones, flashing lights, and a sign that says, "BRIDGE OUT, TURN BACK"—but all you can do is speed up. Why are some people drawn into these kinds of relationships? Why do others stay in them against their better judgment? Here is a list of the top five reasons why people ignore red flags:

> **Fears hold a lot of power when they are kept in secret.**

1. It's familiar to them. Sometimes people get into unhealthy relationships because it is all they know. Perhaps they've witnessed unhealthy relationships in their family. They are simply drawn to what is familiar.

2. They don't deserve anything better. Certain people grow up with an incredible sense of inferiority, a lack of self-respect, or a guilt that leads to the belief that they deserve nothing but the worst in life. This is often the result of childhood neglect or abuse. Sadly, we've known people, for example, who actually believe they deserve to be hit or demeaned. No matter how much you try to reason with them, they can't intellectualize their way out of it. It requires intensive professional counseling.

3. It's better than nothing. Some people actually make a conscious decision to stay in a "red-flag" relationship because they feel they get something valuable out of it. They often reason their way around the problem, knowing full well there is a concern, by saying to themselves, "I know this is a serious concern, but I'm willing to take my chances because it's better than being alone." What's the old saying? "Some attention—even if it's negative—is better than none at all." We don't believe anything could be worth the pain that is associated with any of the five deadly signs.

4. *They have the same problem.* It's hard to take a good look at someone and identify problems when you've got the same problem. For example, maybe you both smoke pot, or you both hate your parents. If the two of you struggle with the same things, be careful not to live blinded by one another's denial of the problem.

5. *Fear of breakup.* Many people stay in sick relationships against their better judgment because of any number of fears: fear of being alone; fear of the unknown; fear of the hurt and loss associated with breaking up; and fear that your boyfriend or girlfriend may do something crazy or irrational. Unfortunately, these fears hold a lot of power when they are kept in secret. Thus, it is critical to verbalize your fears to others. Share them with a parent, trusted friend, pastor, or counselor.

Perhaps this chapter seems to reek of gloom and doom to you, but you don't have to treat these scenarios as your fate. We are making you aware of the warning signs so that you can eventually forge a *healthy* relationship. If you want, try compiling your own list of signs that indicate a relationship is going well. Your own personal list will help you remember exactly what it is that you value in a relationship.

Consequences of Breaking This Commandment

- You risk the possibility of sinking into abusive, unhealthy, and destructive relationships.

- Your self-esteem will be damaged as you continue in a relationship that lacks mutual respect.
- You waste a whole lot of time and energy on an unhealthy relationship.

Benefits of Keeping This Commandment

- You'll avoid heartache and pain.
- You'll avoid the risk of enduring abuse and addiction in your relationships.
- You'll have time to enjoy happier, more fulfilling friendships with people you are compatible with.

Help for You Who Have Broken This Commandment

- Realize that God wants the very best for you.
- Look long and hard at the red flags. Run! Get out!
- Learn from this experience. Be wise in future dating choices.

Still Don't Believe Us? Check This Out:

- "Listen to my teaching, and you will be wise; do not ignore it" (Prov. 8:33).
- "You will teach me how to live a holy life. Being with you will fill me with joy" (Ps. 16:11).
- "If you go the wrong way—to the right or to the left—you will hear a voice behind you saying, 'This is the right way. You should go this way'" (Isa. 30:21).

Thou Shalt Choose Wisely

Remember the movie *Indiana Jones and the Last Crusade*? Indiana Jones, played by Harrison Ford, and an evil character named Donovan are searching for the Holy Grail, the supposed fountain of youth. At the end of the movie, Indiana and Donovan find the room where the grail is being protected by a seven-hundred-year-old knight. They have to pick the right grail from a selection of about twenty-five. The knight tells them both that if they choose the right grail they will have eternal life. If they choose the wrong grail? Eternal damnation.

Donovan gets his sexy, blonde sidekick to make his choice. She impulsively grabs the most beautiful and shiny of the chalices and hands it to Donovan. He holds the cup high and says, "Surely this is the cup of the King of kings." He dips the grail into a pool of water and quickly gulps it down. After breathing a sigh of relief, positive that he has chosen the right cup, he notices the reflection of his face in the pool. Suddenly, he begins to age and wrinkle, his hair grows out, and his entire face rots, turns into a skeleton, and explodes across the screen. After Donovan disintegrates before their very eyes, fragmenting into thousands of pieces, the old knight slowly turns to Indiana and the woman and says, "He chose . . . *poorly*."

How many guys and girls have had their hearts torn apart in the dating process? Why do so many teenagers have a ton of regrets in their love lives? It's partly because they are simply choosing poorly! They're selecting the wrong people to date.

Face it, you can make a lot of poor decisions in your life, and still recover. Believe us, we've been there and done that. You can select the wrong car and trade it in after a few months. You can choose the wrong college and transfer if you don't like it. You can pick the wrong major and revise it later. You can take the wrong job but later land another that you like better. You can make horrible grades one semester but study harder and improve your grades the next. You can move in with a psycho room-

> **If you date and then marry the wrong person, you will live with significant, negative, and lasting consequences of that decision for the rest of your life.**

mate and move out before he or she scars you for life. All of these decisions may carry some adverse consequences but pale in comparison to the consequences of bad decision making in a relationship.

If you don't remember anything else in this book, remember this: *If you date and then marry the wrong person, you will live with significant, negative, and lasting consequences of that decision for the rest of your life.* Marriage may seem like a far-off prospect for the distant future, but remember—*you will eventually marry someone you date!* If you keep choosing poorly in the dating arena, ultimately one of those choices may affect every area of your life. Ouch.

Are You Making Poor Choices?

Donovan made the wrong choice for several reasons: he was impulsive and desperate, he allowed the "sexy blonde" to influence his choice, and, finally, he assumed that this choice was the best based on the external beauty of the chalice. Just as Donovan chose poorly in his quest for the Holy Grail, so do scores of people during their dating life. We have identified three of the more common reasons people make poor dating choices. Each of these reasons keeps them from discerning the true character of the person they are dating. Take a look at these barriers to discerning true character.

1. The "I've-Gotta-Have-Somebody" Syndrome

When you don't know what you are looking for and you are desperate or starved for love, you wind up compromising your standards and settling for the first available warm body. We call this the "I've-Gotta-Have-Somebody" syndrome. Do you ever get super hungry, go to your favorite restaurant, and when the hostess asks, "Do you want smoking, nonsmoking, or first available?" you're so hungry you couldn't care less, so you just respond, "Please give me *first available!*" Many people are so love hungry that they are willing to take the first available guy or girl who comes along. As radio shrink Dr. Laura Schlessinger says, "They become beggars, not choosers" in the dating process.

Allison fell into the "I've-Gotta-Have-Somebody" syndrome when all of her friends began dating someone, and she started to feel like a third wheel wherever she went. Desperate to fit in with the rest of her friends (and have a date for her senior prom), she started going out with a guy she had nothing in common with. She didn't even like him that much. The relationship dragged on for a few weeks before Allison realized she was just dating to be dating. She decided that in future relationships she would be a chooser and not a beggar when it came to the opposite sex. It's okay not to date! You're young—enjoy your freedom. And when it comes time for more serious dating, know what you want, and more importantly, know what you *need* before you ever go out.

2. Fooled by the Externals

Have you ever purchased something off the Internet and really regretted it? If your experience is like some folks', what you end up with is not at all like the picture you saw online. Many of us have experienced the stomach-churning trauma of opening that UPS box only to discover that what we ended up getting was nothing like what we thought we'd ordered. And by the way, you ordered from a site where all sales are *final*. Chalk up another one to deceiving appearances.

> **It's okay not to date! You're young—enjoy your freedom.**

Nearly every week in counseling sessions or on the radio, we ask the all-important question: "What are you looking for in a member of the opposite sex?" By far, most people will initially say, "Well, I'm looking for a person with a good personality, someone who is outdoorsy, funny, good-looking, has a great body, . . . " And they go on and on, listing a host of superficial characteristics and personality traits.

We call this the "Cotton Candy" approach. At a fair or circus your attention gets snagged by the cotton candy vendor. Cotton candy is colorful, beautiful, and looks like a mountain of sweetness. Then you stuff a wad in your mouth and it just melts away. Oh sure, it's sweet, but you paid five dollars for this huge thing that vanishes in seconds, leaving you unsatisfied.

Don't get us wrong—personality and common interests are important—but alone they won't build a lasting relationship. Gazing at the externals may fool you.

3. Blinded by Sex

The Bible says, "Love covers a multitude of sins," but when it comes to dating relationships, sex covers a multitude of flaws. Sex has a way of blinding you from seeing your boyfriend's or girlfriend's true colors. You miss the negative stuff and see only what makes you feel good.

Sex is great in the right context (marriage), but in dating relationships it clouds the relationship and shuts down communication. Guys usually mistake the lovemaking for love itself. In other words, they think that if you have sex, you don't need anything else. Girls, on the other hand, have a tendency to confuse sex with commitment. They think that the guy somehow values this relationship as unique and special. A girl will think to herself, *This must really mean love.* Come on, girls, wake up! Some guys will potentially make love with anyone, anyway, anytime, anywhere, for just about any reason under the right circumstances. So, whether it's trading sex for love or love for sex, the sexual relationship is not only *wrong,* but it also gives a false sense of closeness, blinding both parties from seeing the real person they are dating.

If you desire to make wise dating choices, then know what you want so that you won't just settle for the "first available," and make sure your focus is on the internals (like the Essential Character Qualities you are about to discover). And remember to take it slow and save sex for marriage.

Discerning Character

This final section could be summed up with one phrase: Dating is discernment. The dating experience is about being able to discern who this person really is. *Webster's Collegiate Dictionary* expresses this idea perfectly: Discernment is "the quality of being able to grasp and comprehend what is obscure . . . a searching that goes beyond the obvious or superficial." Think about it. That's precisely the goal of dating.

But the dating practices of our culture really are quite bizarre. You hide your true self behind your outward appearance—wearing just the right clothes, the right fragrance, saying the right thing at the right time, and trying to somehow be who you think this other person wants you to be. In other cultures, the parents play a primary role in picking out marriage partners for their children, and the game playing is kept to a minimum. While we could certainly benefit from adapting some practices of other cultures, we aren't interested in telling you to "kiss dating good-bye," as some have suggested. So, we're stuck with the tremendous challenge to get beyond the masks and discover the true person underneath. Your job is to penetrate this natural tendency to impress and gain insight into who they *really* are. Ultimately, you're trying to discern character.

What Is Character?

If you could strip away the physical attributes, the clothes, the polite sayings, even the charming personality, everything that remains comprises character. Character is basically who you are when no one is looking. Because of our culture's emphasis on style over substance, character, by its very nature, cannot be perceived very quickly. The task of discerning character is a long-term process. You can't expect to know one's insides really without seeing that person in many different settings and under many different circumstances.

> **Character is basically who you are when no one is looking.**

So what makes up good character in the person you date? We have identified five *Essential Character Qualities* (ECQs) that you should look for: faithful, honest, committed, forgiving, and giving. You will find these to be extremely obvious and yet so often overlooked. Let's take a closer look at these qualities.

1. Faithful

A faithful person is loyal and can demonstrate an allegiance to others. As you observe this person in his friendships and family relationships does he pass the test of loyalty? Is this someone who keeps her promises? Does he know how to really care about someone, even when the going gets tough?

2. Honest

An honest person is genuine and free of deception. This quality of honesty encompasses three aspects: words, actions, and personhood. First, it has to do with his word. Can you trust him to tell you the truth? Does he mean what he says? Is he prone to lies or deception (even "white" lies)? Second, honesty involves actions and behavior. Does he act with integrity? Do others consider him to be credible, reputable, and respectable? Finally, does he have the capacity to be real, genuine, and transparent? How difficult is it to know this person? Are you able to discern his inner qualities over a period of time, or does this person have so many layers of defenses and disguises that you cannot penetrate?

3. Committed

The idea here is to find someone who can demonstrate a lifestyle of commitment, not someone who just talks about his commitment. Anybody can say, "Yes, I'm committed." But do they really have what it takes to be committed to something for the long haul? Are they committed to people, projects, and organizations, even when the fun gave out a long time ago?

4. Forgiving

Forgiveness is simply releasing a person from the debt you perceive they owe you. It is about letting go of the need to punish, resent, or hold grudges when you have been wronged. If you are serious about finding someone with the character trait of forgiveness, make sure they know about the ten magic words: "I am sorry. I was wrong. Will you forgive me?" If you don't know why these words possess a little bit of magic, go try them out for yourself. What kind of person are you dating? Is he quick to condemn and slow to release others off the hook? Does he hold grudges or resentment? How does he resolve conflicts? Do you see an eagerness to compromise, let go, and move forward? Is there evidence of a forgiving spirit? We hope so. A successful relationship between two imperfect people must be bathed in mutual forgiveness.

5. Giving

This quality is not about giving material gifts but, rather, the capacity for selfless behavior. Giving means putting others first. A giver gets outside of himself and gives to others rather than always seeking to get something *from* them. Such a person has the capacity to be "other-centered." He can demonstrate sensitivity to people's needs and the ability to meet those needs. Most important, a giver desires to see you grow and to love you in a way that promotes wholeness. When the romantic love fades (which indeed it will), a relationship can be sustained only by a deeper kind of love, the kind that seeks to see you grow.

Helpful Hints for Discerning Character

1. Tough Times Reveal Someone's True Character

When someone is faced with a difficult circumstance or crisis situation, he usually doesn't have time to think. At crucial moments when a sudden decision must be made, people do what comes natural. They respond from the heart. Pay close attention to people under pressure or in crisis situations if you want to know their true colors.

2. Character Is Who You Are When No One Is Looking

If this is true, then it is vital that you place a heavy emphasis on your boyfriend's or girlfriend's behavior when you are alone. The way you are treated by him or her in private is far more important than how you are treated in public, particularly around family and friends. Many can fake character in public, and some are fabulous actors when the occasion calls for it. So if you find yourself being treated by your boyfriend or girlfriend in a manner that is inappropriate or disrespectful in front of others, what does that say about this person's true character? You can bet it's even worse.

3. Friends Are a Window into a Person's Character

To really know someone, take a look at his friends. What kind of people does he hang out with? We all tend to gravitate toward those with whom we feel we have a lot in common. Furthermore, we usually become like those with whom we associate. Consider what the apostle Paul says in 1 Corinthians 15:33, "Do not be misled: 'Bad company corrupts good character'" (NIV). Rarely does the influence occur the other way around.

4. Look at the Person's Other Relationships to Determine Patterns of Behavior

Consider whether there is a pattern of disloyalty, dishonesty, or unkindness in other relationships. Pay attention to how they talk about or treat their parents, siblings, or teachers. Often this will give you clues as to who a person really is. In the final analysis, behavior patterns reveal more than words or promises.

5. Give It Lots of Time

One of the points we have continued to stress throughout is the need to give yourself a lot of time in order to discover who this other person truly is. It's such an obvious truth and yet so difficult to do. It would be hard to exaggerate the importance of this truth. In fact, we devoted a whole chapter to this matter (Commandment Four, "Thou Shalt Take It Slow").

It's Your Choice

In the conclusion of *Indiana Jones and the Last Crusade*, Donovan had "chosen poorly" in his quest for the grail, and it was finally Indiana's turn to make a choice from the many chalices set before him. Remember, he bypassed the shiny, ornate, and richly adorned goblets—those that were initially pleasing to the eye. Instead, he chose a simple, worn, and nondescript cup that, when dipped into the water, revealed itself to be solid gold. Indiana drank of the cup, and the knight affirmed, "You chose *wisely*." Don't miss the point. We're not saying that you need to find someone with tarnished looks and a dusty personality. Rather, seek to be discriminating about the character of the person you choose to date. Don't compromise in this crucial area. If there is ever a time to be picky, this is it! All of these qualities should be *nonnegotiable*. Too often we see individuals who are willing to compromise and accept three or four out of five of these qualities. These odds sound good in Las Vegas but don't hold up to the necessary requirements for a healthy relationship.

Most, if not all, of the pop songs played on the radio imply that all you need is love. This directly violates the Law of Choosing Wisely. The subtle message is, "Don't be discriminating; just be glad you've got someone who loves you. Don't worry about someone's past or what is on the inside—that's all irrelevant as long as he or she loves you." What a joke! The only way to choose wisely is to make choices based upon character—those intangible qualities. It's okay to have your "wish list" of characteristics you want in a mate, but make sure your primary focus is on what you need—good character. Here's the bottom line. When discerning character, ask yourself five simple questions:

1. Can he or she demonstrate loyalty?
2. Can he or she be open and real?
3. Can he or she hang in when the going gets tough?

4. Can he or she let you off the hook?

5. Can he or she put you first?

Consequences of Breaking This Commandment

- You may eventually marry someone who is attractive, rich, and funny, but you will be unhappy and unfulfilled because he or she isn't what you really need.

- You may live through the pain and brokenness of a relationship that has gone asunder, all because you chose to become involved with the wrong person and eventually married someone who is lazy, dishonest, unfaithful, or spiritually uncommitted.

Benefits of Keeping This Commandment

- You will greatly increase your odds of getting what you want.

- You will greatly improve your chances of being in a healthy relationship.

- You will bypass losers early on in the dating process, thus saving time, energy, and money.

- You will become a chooser instead of a beggar in the dating game.

Help for You Who Have Broken This Commandment

- If you are currently in a relationship and you know this is not what you need or want, get out of the relationship now. Assume that nothing will change this person. If you kiss a toad, you simply get slime in your mouth.

- If you are not attached, dating, or even "hanging out" with anyone in particular, then make a commitment to look for the five ECQs in all future relationships.

Still Don't Believe Us? Check This Out:

- "Keep your eyes focused on what is right, and look straight ahead to what is good" (Prov. 4:25).

- "My child, hold on to wisdom and good sense. Don't let them out of your sight. They will give you life and beauty like a necklace around your neck. Then you will go your way in safety, and you will not get hurt" (Prov. 3:21–23).

- "Delight yourself also in the LORD, and He shall give you the desires of your heart" (Ps. 37:4 NKJV).

Commandment 10

Thou Shalt Take Action

You were drawn to this book for a reason. Obviously, you want God's best for your dating life, and you desire a healthy relationship when the time is right. In order for this to happen, though, you must apply what you've learned. There is nothing worse than reading this book, agreeing with what we say, and yet doing nothing about it.

If you haven't figured it out yet, we are very action oriented. We believe that any change in your life must be accompanied by action (literally, physical movement). Having the information alone is just not enough. If you desire to make changes, then there must be a point at which you begin to "move your feet" regardless of whether or not you feel like doing so. Michele Weiner-Davis, a popular self-help author, put it well

> **Any change in your life must be accompanied by action (literally, physical movement).**

when she said that the difference between those who turn their life around and live their dreams, and those who make no change is summed up in one word: action.[1]

As such, we would like to offer several clear-cut methods for taking action now and getting the most out of this material. If you want to gain the most benefit from this book, you must identify which laws you are violating, and then take action. It may require you to break up with the person you are dating because you know he or she isn't right for you. Or you may need to wise-up, take our advice, and start group dating rather than spending so much time alone with the opposite sex. If your standards have slipped in the physical realm, you may want to recommit your life to purity and wholeness. Or maybe you are plagued by low self-esteem or self-doubt, and it is finally time to do something about it. Any of these steps may be difficult, but they are necessary. Do you need to make changes? Are you ready to take action? Then take our advice below.

Do you understand that you have infinite worth and value because you are created in God's image?

Take a Look at Yourself

It all starts with you. No one else can make you happy or whole. No boyfriend or girlfriend can complete you. You must be solid and complete all by yourself. Do you know who you are? Do you feel good about yourself? Do you have a solid sense of worth and value? Do you understand that you have infinite worth and value because you are created in God's image? The answer is either yes or no! If *yes*, then forge ahead and take a look at these next considerations. If you answered *no*, then take deliberate action now! Do something about it. It's that simple. Make it your number one goal to begin to firm up your identity in Christ and deal with this once and for all. You may even want to check out Robert McGee's excellent book, *The Search for Significance*.[2] You may also need the help of your youth pastor, your friends who are seeking God, or your family. (Most likely, you'll need all three.)

Take Responsibility for Your Relationships

If you are the type who constantly finds yourself attracted to and hanging out with losers, it is time to identify the patterns that got you there and resolve to change them. If you find yourself in relationships that are unhealthy or harmful, make a decision to get out. Possibly, you're in a relationship with someone who is disrespectful or critical. Listen, you don't have to be a victim of "bad luck" anymore. It's time to take responsibility for your choices. Quit blaming others, and learn to avoid certain patterns and unhealthy people. You have the power and the courage to make the right decision. And if you need to reach out to others for help and support, then by all means reach out.

Take Your Time and Relax

In case the obvious didn't quite make its way into your noggin, let us reiterate one of the underlying themes: *Take it slow, get to know*. Hopefully you understand the importance of going slow during this time of your life. We can't possibly overstate the value of guarding your heart, protecting your body, and avoiding "serious" relationships. On the other hand, there may be some reading this book who have never dated anyone. You may be wondering, *Will I ever meet someone worth dating?* Or *Why does love seem to happen to everyone but me?* Our response:

Don't rush! Enjoy having friends of both sexes; there will be plenty of time for more serious stuff later. And now that you've read this book, you'll save yourself a lot of heartache when you do start dating.

Take Back What You Lost

This is yet another group made up of people who have been devastated or wounded due to repeated violations of one or a combination of commandments. For example, many of us have succumbed to the temptation of going too fast in a relationship. It's easy to speed when you are excited about someone. At one time or another, many of us have been guilty of putting too much emphasis on the romantic/passionate aspect of a relationship (in other words, we failed to use our brain). Sadly, some of us can even relate to the regrets associated with sexual indiscretion. Perhaps you have lost your confidence, dignity, or self-respect. Well, it's time to take back what you may have lost. It's never too late to start fresh and remember that God overflows with grace, forgiveness, and unconditional love. However, *it is up to you* to start the process of healing through acknowledgment, confession, and renewal.

Take Time Out

Whenever you do find yourself strongly attracted to someone, you must take time out to consider the fruit of that relationship. There is one simple question that can help you determine whether or not you should hang out with this person: Is this an affirming kind of relationship? In other words, are you encouraging each other to grow and become better people as a result of the relationship? If so, there will be mutual respect and it will be characterized by agape love—not motivated by selfishness.

Take These Laws Seriously

Finally, we want you to remember that these laws are not recommendations or suggestions. Ignore them, and you pay the consequences. We can't always predict or pinpoint a direct result, but we can guarantee it will be negative. On the other hand, seek to follow these laws, and you will experience positive results—blessings! Relationships don't have to be as complicated and mysterious as we sometimes make them. Obey the Ten Commandments of Dating, and you will experience clarity, security, hope, and—most of all—blessing.

Some Final Words of Wisdom

- "You know that in a race all the runners run, but only one gets the prize. So run to win! All those who compete in the games use self-control so they can win a crown. That crown is an earthly thing that lasts only a short time, but our crown will never be destroyed" (1 Cor. 9:24–25).

- "Do not let anyone treat you as if you are unimportant because you are young. Instead, be an example to the believers with your words, your actions, your love, your faith, and your pure life" (1 Tim. 4:12).

Notes

Commandment 1

1. Peter Kreeft, *Knowing the God Who Loves You* (Ann Arbor, MI: Servant Publications, 1988), 171.
2. *How the Grinch Stole Christmas*, Dr. Seuss, 1966, Turner Entertainment Company on Warner Home Video.
3. Leo Buscaglia, *Living, Loving, and Learning* (New York, Ballantine, 1983).

Commandment 6

1. Rick Stedman, *Pure Joy!: The Positive Side of Single Sexuality* (Chicago: Moody Press, 1993), 59–60.
2. STD statistics from Worth the Wait®. Available at http://www.worththewait.org.
3. Mark Sherman, "STDs Unevenly High in Teens, Young Adults," *The Associated Press*, February 24, 2004.

Commandment 7

1. Erika Harold, testimony before the U.S. House of Representatives, April 23, 2002. Available at http://www.projectreality.org.

2. Gary Smith, "Mama's Boys," *Sports Illustrated*, April 23, 2001.

3. Sexual behavior statistics acquired from the Centers for Disease Control, 2003. Available at http://www.cdc.gov/nccdphp/dash/sexualbehaviors/index.htm.

4. Population statistics acquired from the Census Bureau, 2000.

5. Nina Bernstein, "Young Love, New Caution," *New York Times*, sec. 1, March 7, 2004.

6. John Harris, "Why Wait?" presentation, seminar notes, Campus Crusade for Christ (March 1991).

7. David C. Reardon, *Making Abortion Rare* (San Francisco: Acorn Books, 1996), x.

8. M. Bulfin, MD. "A New Problem in Adolescent Gynecology," *Southern Medical Journal,* 72, no. 8 (August 1979).

9. Erika Harold, http://www.projectreality.org.

Commandment 10

1. Michele Weiner-Davis, *Change Your Life and Everyone in It* (New York: Simon & Schuster, 1995), 53.

2. Robert McGee, *The Search for Significance* (Nashville: W Publishing, 2003).

About the Authors

Ben Young, M.Div. leads seminars on how to build successful dating relationships. Former host of *The Single Connection,* a nationally syndicated radio show for singles, Ben is a teaching pastor at the 38,000-member Second Baptist Church in Houston, Texas. For more information, visit www.BenYoung.org.

Sam Adams, Psy.D., is a licensed clinical psychologist. He earned his bachelor's degree from Baylor University. He went on to receive his master's from Western Seminary and a doctorate from George Fox Graduate School of Clinical Psychology. He maintains a full-time counseling practice in Austin, Texas, where his primary emphasis is on relationship and marital issues. He resides in Austin with his wife, Julie, and their four children.

For Speaking Engagements
and Conference Information:

Ben Young
6400 Woodway
Houston, TX 77057
713-465-3408
or you may go to www.BenYoung.org.

For more dating advice . . .

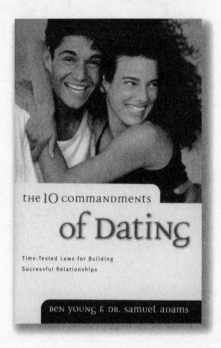

Are you tired of pouring time, energy, and money into relationships that start off great and end with heartache? Maybe you are frustrated because you cannot find "the one" for you, no matter how hard you pray, primp, and plead. If so, you need *The Ten Commandments of Dating* to give you the hard-hitting, black-and-white, practical guidelines that will address your questions and frustrations about dating. This guide will help you keep your head in the search for the desire of your heart.

The Ten Commandments of Dating is not more relationship advice—it's relationship common sense.

The Ten Commandments of Dating

ISBN 0-7852-7022-1

BEN YOUNG & DR. SAMUEL ADAMS

authors of the bestseller THE TEN COMMANDMENTS OF DATING

The One

A REALISTIC GUIDE TO CHOOSING YOUR SOUL MATE

The biggest question on the minds of 78 million singles in America is simply this: "How can I find the right one?" This book answers that question, giving entertaining yet practical advice for that seemingly endless quest to find "The One."

This book emphasizes free will, personal responsibility, proactivity, and preparation, helping singles avoid the pitfalls of dangerous beliefs and hyper-spirituality. Single Christians will learn what approaches to avoid in mate selection, recognize the myths about finding true love, and learn practical strategies for finding the right person to marry.

The One

ISBN 0-7852-6744-1

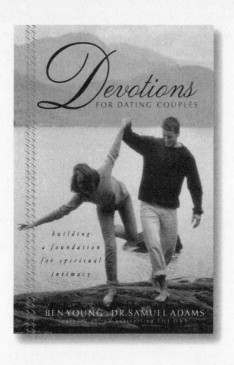

Designed especially for highly committed or engaged couples, this book helps readers: understand and avoid the most common barriers to spiritual growth, have an increased desire for fellowship with God, share and explore spiritual issues together, and pursue godliness, personal relational health, and wholeness.

Each of the nine sections includes Scripture quotations, suggested meditation passages, and discussion questions, as well as anecdotes from real people including the authors. Intended as an eight-week study, weekday devotions are to be completed by both individuals, and each weekend study is to be completed together as a couple.

Devotions for Dating Couples

ISBN 0-7852-6749-2